MARVEL
SPIDER-MAN
CHARACTER ENCYCLOPEDIA

WRITTEN BY
DANIEL WALLACE

INTRODUCTION

The wall-crawling, web-swinging Spider-Man is one of the greatest heroes of them all. Peter Parker, science genius and photographer for *The Daily Bugle*, has secretly protected New York City and the world from a host of Super Villains, such as Doctor Octopus, the Green Goblin, Venom, and the Sinister Six. Meet Spidey's closest friends, including the Avengers and the Fantastic Four, and come face to face with his worst enemies in this one-of-a-kind visual guide.

Contents

This book contains more than 200 characters with links to Spider-Man. Each page is filled with revealing facts. Apart from Peter Parker/Spider-Man – featured in the opening pages – characters appear in alphabetical order according to their first names. Some characters, such as Norman Osborn, whose significance goes far beyond the Green Goblin, have two entries. Use the contents list below to swing straight to the Super Hero or Villain of your choice.

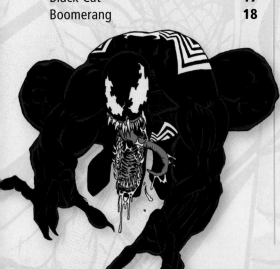

PETER PARKER

Having the secret identity of Spider-Man has caused Peter Parker plenty of headaches, but he knows it's the only way to keep his loved ones safe. Peter has worked as a photographer for *The Daily Bugle* and as a researcher for Horizon Labs. Mary Jane Watson and Peter's beloved Aunt May are two of the most important people in his life.

Peter never expected that the bite of a radioactive spider would react with his DNA and turn him into the amazing Spider-Man.

WEB FILE

In addition to his spider-powers, Peter Parker is a scientific genius with a talent for mechanical engineering and physics. He is also a skilled photographer.

— POWER RATING —

Intelligence	●●●●●●○
Strength	●●●●●○○
Speed	●●●○○○○
Durability	●●●●○○○
Energy Projection	●○○○○○○
Fighting Skill	●●●●●○○

Brains and Hard Work

Peter has always struggled for money. For years he supported his Aunt May with his earnings from *The Daily Bugle*, and he has also used his engineering talents to earn money on the side. Peter doesn't accept payment for his work as Spider-Man.

As a photographer, Peter dresses in clothing that won't draw attention.

SPIDER-MAN

WEB FILE

Spider-Man can cling to most surfaces and has superhuman strength, speed and reflexes. "Spider-sense" warns him of danger. Wrist web-shooters spray strong web-lines.

— POWER RATING —

Intelligence ●●●●●○○
Strength ●●●●●○○
Speed ●●●○○○○
Durability ●●●○○○○
Energy Projection ●○○○○○○
Fighting Skill ●●●○○○○

Shy teenager Peter Parker gained super powers from a radioactive spider, and discovered that with great power comes great responsibility! The death of his Uncle Ben inspired Peter to protect the weak as Spider-Man, the wall-crawling, web-swinging protector of New York City.

Hero or Menace?

Spider-Man is a misunderstood figure in the city he calls home, thanks to the negative press coverage of J. Jonah Jameson and *The Daily Bugle*. Yet he never gives up, and is good friends with well-respected teams such as the Avengers and the Fantastic Four.

Spidey's web shooters are mechanical devices.

Spidey swings high above New York City, his home and base of operations for Super Hero adventures.

Spider-Man has perfect control over his wall-crawling grip.

"Just watch and see what I can do!"

SPIDER-MAN'S COSTUMES

Peter Parker made his first red-and-blue costume himself. Since then, new challenges have brought new changes! Spider-Man's black-and-white costume was later revealed to be the alien symbiote Venom. Other variants include a Horizon Labs stealth suit and the "Iron Spider" armour designed by Tony Stark.

COSTUMES

1. **Spider Armour:** Bulletproof suit made from flexible metal.

2. **Black Suit:** Revealed to be an alien symbiote in disguise.

3. **Iron Spider Armour:** Advanced suit with targeting systems and four extendible arms.

4. **Stealth Suit:** Bends light and sound around its wearer.

SPIDER-MAN'S IDENTITIES

Framed by Norman Osborn for a crime he didn't commit, Spider-Man couldn't show himself in public without getting arrested. Instead, he created four new personas – the jet-powered Hornet, the shadowy Dusk, the nimble Ricochet and the heroic Prodigy – to provide cover while he worked to clear his name.

IDENTITIES

1. **Prodigy:** Powerful, muscular hero showcasing Spidey's superhuman strength.

2. **Dusk:** Secretive observer showcasing Spidey's spider-sense.

3. **Ricochet:** Quick-moving wise-cracker showcasing Spidey's amazing agility.

4. **Hornet:** Armoured, flying hero, employing a costume with a cybernetically controlled jetpack.

ALIEN SYMBIOTE

Parasites from beyond the stars, the alien symbiotes have bonded with human hosts to become some of Spider-Man's most fearsome enemies – Venom, Carnage, Scream and more. These shape-changers cover their hosts head to toe and feed off their emotions, while also giving them superhuman abilities.

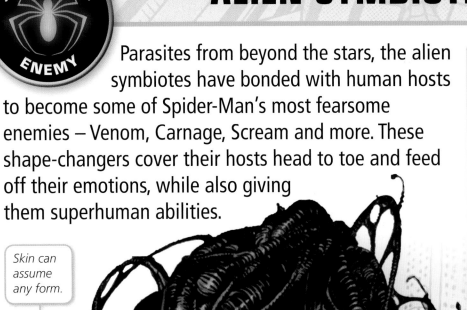

Skin can assume any form.

Separated from its host body, a symbiote is still dangerous – it can move and attack on its own.

Secrets of the Species

The symbiotes are conquerors who lack feelings of their own. Instead, they drain the emotions of others, especially fear and hatred. They force their hosts into deadly situations where they will experience fear. Another alien species, the Xenophage, is their natural enemy.

Fangs can sometimes inject venom.

WEB FILE

Symbiotes give their hosts superhuman strength, speed and agility. They can also control the actions of their hosts.

— POWER RATING —

Intelligence	●●●●●●○
Strength	●●●●●●●
Speed	●●●○○○○
Durability	●●●●●○○
Energy Projection	●●○○○○○
Fighting Skill	●●●●○○○

ALISTAIR SMYTHE

WEB FILE

Alistair Smythe's Ultimate Spider-Slayer bio-organic suit gives him superhuman strength and features built-in cutting blades and web-shooters.

— POWER RATING —

Intelligence ●●●●●●●
Strength ●●●●●●●
Speed ●●●●○○○
Durability ●●●●●○○
Energy Projection ●●●○○○○
Fighting Skill ●●●●○○○

Like father, like son! After Alistair Smythe's father, Spencer Smythe, died while trying to eliminate Spider-Man with his Spider-Slayer robots, Alistair continued his family's tradition of terror. Alistair designed a new generation of Spider-Slayer robots, and fought the web-slinger while wearing an armoured suit as the Ultimate Spider-Slayer.

"It's called Hobson's choice, Spider-Man. Who will you save?"

Bio-organic armour protects against energy blasts.

Driven by hatred, Alistair has transformed himself into a fearsome foe.

Metal Menace
Alistair has sought revenge on Spider-Man and J. Jonah Jameson, blaming them for his father's death. To prolong his life, he has become a cyborg by merging his body with the mechanical components of his Spider-Slayer robots.

ANTI-VENOM

When Eddie Brock removed the alien symbiote called Venom from his body, tiny traces of it remained. These remnants, mutated by the healing powers of Mister Negative, bonded with Eddie's white blood cells to create Anti-Venom. Despite their long history as enemies, he and Spider-Man joined forces.

Anti-Venom's intentions may be good, but his appearance is fearsome, and people fear alien symbiotes like him.

Healing and Helping

Eddie Brock has worked hard to make up for the crimes he committed as Venom. Anti-Venom's healing abilities saved the day when New York's citizens suddenly gained spider powers, and the city descended into chaos as "Spider-Island".

"You are diseased! And only my touch can save you!"

Senses are sharper than any human's.

Touch can transfer healing microbes.

WEB FILE

Anti-Venom has superhuman strength, durability and stamina, as well as incredible healing powers. He can wall-crawl and shoot out parts of himself in the form of webs or tentacles.

— POWER RATING —

Intelligence	●●●●●●○
Strength	●●●●●●○
Speed	●●●○○○○
Durability	●●●●●●○
Energy Projection	●●●●○○○
Fighting Skill	●●●●●●○

AUNT MAY PARKER

Peter Parker's kindly Aunt May has been like a mother to him since he was a boy. When her husband, Ben Parker, was killed by a burglar, Aunt May raised Peter on her own as he secretly started his life as a Super Hero. She has since learned the truth about his double identity, and is always there to support him in his role as Spider-Man.

Being close to Peter has often placed Aunt May in danger.

Aunt May is a practical, down-to-earth homemaker. Losing his parents, and later his Uncle Ben, taught Peter to value the role that she plays in his life.

"Now and forever, I'll be right here."

Life Changes
Aunt May later married Jay Jameson, father of *The Daily Bugle's* J. Jonah Jameson. She and her new husband made the tough decision to move from New York City to Boston, but Aunt May still keeps in touch with Peter.

Learning Peter's secret didn't change Aunt May's love for him.

WEB FILE
Aunt May has no special combat skills or super powers, but she is a smart, resourceful woman and an excellent judge of character.

— POWER RATING —
Intelligence ●●●●○○○
Strength ●○○○○○○
Speed ●○○○○○○
Durability ●○○○○○○
Energy Projection ●○○○○○○
Fighting Skill ●●○○○○○

AVENGERS

With a cry of "Avengers Assemble," the world's greatest Super Hero team races into action! The Avengers take on Super Villains that are too powerful for a single hero to defeat. At first, Spider-Man was a reserve member. When the team reformed as the New Avengers, he joined full-time.

KEY MEMBERS

1. **Captain America:** Indestructible shield.

2. **Wolverine:** Claws, healing powers.

3. **Hulk:** Incredible strength and durability.

4. **Falcon:** Wings allow him to fly at hundreds of miles per hour

5. **Black Widow:** Gauntlets fire high-voltage electrostatic bolts.

6. **Thor:** Wields the mystical Asgardian hammer Mjolnir.

7. **Human Torch:** Controls fire and can fly.

8. **Iron Man:** Armored battlesuit.

Recruiting Drive

Early in their history, the Avengers tried to recruit Spider-Man as a potential new member. As part of the initiation test they asked Spidey to capture the Hulk! Spider-Man refused membership at the time, but continued to work with the Avengers on a reserve basis for years.

"We'll never be beaten, for we are the Avengers!"

The Avengers excel at stealth, combat, and tactics.

BASILISK

Basil Elks got no respect as a common criminal, but a close encounter with an alien artifact called the Alpha Stone mutated him into a super-powered reptile. As the Basilisk, Elks fought Spider-Man and sought out the Alpha Stone's counterpart, the Omega Stone, to gain even more power.

Like the mythological monster of the same name, Basilisk can freeze others in their tracks – even agile foes like Spider-Man.

"Fools laughed at me in prison, but they'll never laugh again!"

Making His Mark

Having endured the mockery of his fellow criminals, Basilisk relished his new role as a powerful villain. He suffered many defeats when facing off against Spider-Man, and eventually met his end at the hands of the vigilante Scourge. Years later, he was brought back to life by the villain known as the Hood.

Incredibly tough skin.

Augmented muscles boost strength.

WEB FILE

Basilisk projects microwave energy blasts from his eyes to heat or freeze targets or to levitate them. He can also teleport and has superhuman strength and durability.

— POWER RATING —

Intelligence	●●●●○○○○
Strength	●●●●●○○○
Speed	●●●○○○○○
Durability	●●●●●●○○
Energy Projection	●●●●●●○○
Fighting Skill	●●●●○○○○

BEETLE

Mechanical genius Abner Jenkins built a flying suit of armour and became the costumed criminal Beetle. He clashed with Spider-Man before masquerading as a hero in the Thunderbolts team – and discovering that he actually preferred being good. Abner took the identity of MACH-1, leaving others to carry on the legacy of the Beetle.

Concealed within the armored gauntlets are energy weapons.

"Hold still, blast you!"

Beetle is constantly upgrading his suit to put himself in a better position for fighting super-powered monsters.

Sky High
Before he launched his criminal career, Abner Jenkins worked as an aircraft mechanic. He put his aviation knowledge to good use when designing his flying suit, allowing the Beetle to run rings around non-airborne heroes like Spider-Man.

Costume is lightweight but also completely bulletproof.

WEB FILE

Beetle's battle armor has an arsenal of weaponry and gives him the powers of a jet fighter, with superhuman strength, durability and flight, thanks to a winged, jet-powered harness.

POWER RATING

Intelligence	●●●●●●○○○
Strength	●●●●○○○○○
Speed	●●●●●●○○○
Durability	●●●●●○○○○
Energy Projection	●●●●●○○○○
Fighting Skill	●●●●●●○○○

14

BETTY BRANT

As secretary to *The Daily Bugle* editor J. Jonah Jameson, Betty Brant spent a lot of time with Peter Parker. This closeness led to a brief romance, until Betty thought that Peter liked Liz Allen better. Betty became an investigative reporter, and is still one of Peter's closest friends.

Betty carries recording equipment with her at all times in case a news story breaks.

Dressed for a night on the town.

Her history with Spider-Man has often put Betty in the line of fire, but close encounters with Super Villains have also made her stronger.

Putting the Past Behind Her

Betty dated *The Daily Bugle* reporter Ned Leeds, and the two eventually married. Their rocky marriage ended when Ned was murdered by criminals, and many wrongly believed that Ned had been the criminal Hobgoblin. Afterwards, Betty threw herself into her work, becoming a skilled and respected investigative journalist.

"Peter, you're my only good friend."

WEB FILE

Betty is an excellent journalist, one of *The Daily Bugle*'s finest. She is also skilled at various martial arts.

—— POWER RATING ——

Intelligence	●●●●●○○○○○
Strength	●●○○○○○○○○
Speed	●●○○○○○○○○
Durability	●●●○○○○○○○
Energy Projection	●○○○○○○○○○
Fighting Skill	●●●●○○○○○○

BIG MAN

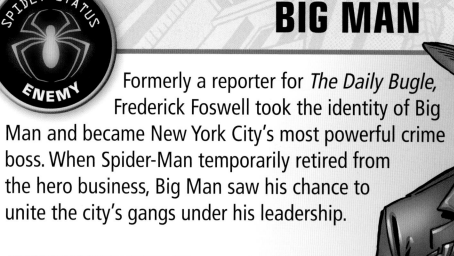

Formerly a reporter for *The Daily Bugle*, Frederick Foswell took the identity of Big Man and became New York City's most powerful crime boss. When Spider-Man temporarily retired from the hero business, Big Man saw his chance to unite the city's gangs under his leadership.

Big Man concealed his identity from his closest allies.

Weapons are hidden in pockets.

Big Man's mask concealed his true identity and allowed others to continue in the role after his demise.

"I'm taking over all the rackets in the city!"

A special suit made Big Man appear larger than he really was.

WEB FILE

Big Man was a criminal mastermind. His padded costume increased his size and he wore a mask fitted with a voice-deepening device. He was a crack shot and a master of disguise.

— POWER RATING —

Intelligence ●●●●●○○○○○
Strength ●●○○○○○○○○
Speed ●●●○○○○○○○
Durability ●●●○○○○○○○
Energy Projection ●○○○○○○○○○
Fighting Skill ●●●●○○○○○○

Big Problems

Big Man climbed up the rungs of the criminal ladder until he rivalled the Kingpin. But he died when he took a bullet meant for J. Jonah Jameson. His daughter Janice briefly became the new Big Man, causing further headaches for Spider-Man.

BLACK CAT

WEB FILE

Black Cat has various devices in her costume that give her extra strength, speed and agility. Her gloves have retractable claws, and she is an Olympic level athlete and martial artist.

— POWER RATING —

Intelligence ●●●●●●●○○○
Strength ●●●●○○○○○○
Speed ●●●○○○○○○○
Durability ●●●●○○○○○○
Energy Projection ●○○○○○○○○○
Fighting Skill ●●●●●○○○○○

Black Cat used to be a professional cat burglar, and she still has a wild side. She and Spider-Man once dated, which inspired her to become a more heroic person. Since then her acrobatic skills have made her a valuable member of hero teams. She knows the secret of Peter Parker's dual identity, but he trusts her completely.

Cat-claw grappling hooks are used to scale buildings.

A Tricky Gift

The Black Cat possesses the ability to manipulate the probability field in her immediate surroundings, bringing cases of inexplicable "bad luck" on her friends and enemies alike. With practice, she has learned to use this field as a weapon.

Despite their friendship, Spider-Man and the Black Cat have often found themselves on opposite sides.

The Black Cat's costume contains various eavesdropping devices.

BOOMERANG

Fred Myers moved from Australia to America as a small child. He used his skills as a baseball pitcher to become an assassin for hire, and tried to win favour with the crime lord Kingpin by killing Spider-Man. When that failed, he found a new way to threaten the wall-crawler by joining the Sinister Syndicate.

While skilled at throwing and catching his own weapons, Boomerang is able to avoid most projectiles aimed at him.

"You're now facing a true craftsman in the art of assassination!"

Selling his Skills

Originally recruited by a secret society to serve as their armed agent, Boomerang later pursued a freelance criminal career. With a deadly aim and an arsenal of throwing weapons, Boomerang has had no trouble attracting paying clients.

His weapons always come back to him, but Boomerang keeps spares on his costume just in case.

Excellent agility compensates for a lack of superpowers.

WEB FILE

Boomerang is an expert with a variety of boomerangs that contain explosives ("shatterangs"), gas ("gasarangs") or have razor-sharp edges ("razorangs").

— POWER RATING —

Intelligence	●●●●○○○
Strength	●●●○○○○
Speed	●●●○○○○
Durability	●●●○○○○
Energy Projection	○○○○○○○
Fighting Skill	●●●●○○○

CAPTAIN AMERICA

WEB FILE

With his body honed to physical perfection by the Super-Soldier serum, Captain America is a superb gymnast, an expert military strategist and a martial arts master.

—— POWER RATING ——

Intelligence	●●●●●●○○
Strength	●●●●○○○○
Speed	●●○○○○○○
Durability	●●●●●○○○
Energy Projection	●○○○○○○○
Fighting Skill	●●●●●●●○

As Captain America, Steve Rogers is a living legend. During World War II he was given a special serum that transformed him into a superhuman soldier. He fought the evil Nazi Red Skull, and after decades frozen in suspended animation, he became one of the founding members of the Avengers.

Cap's indestructible vibranium shield doubles as a throwing weapon.

In every grouping of the Avengers, including the one to which Spider-Man belongs, Captain America is the team's heart and soul.

True Leadership
Captain America is a veteran with decades of experience as a hero, but he has often expressed his respect for the much younger Spider-Man. Cap and Spidey have served together with the New Avengers, and teamed up to defeat the villain known as Queen.

CARDIAC

Dr. Elias Wirtham became the vigilante Cardiac after a medical tragedy led to his brother's death. Transforming his body with cybernetic surgery, Cardiac set out to punish those he blamed. Cardiac considers himself a hero, but he often finds Spider-Man standing in the way of his ruthless revenge plots.

"Tell the slime you work for, Cardiac is here!"

Spider-Man doesn't kill criminals, and tries to stop vigilantes like Cardiac who don't share his outlook.

War of Ideals

Cardiac's crusade has put him up against villains and heroes alike. He stole a device to help a girl with brain damage, forcing him into conflict with Doctor Octopus, who had taken on the role of Spider-Man. Luckily, Cardiac was able to convince Doc Ock to perform the surgery that saved the girl's life.

Vibranium suit absorbs impacts.

WEB FILE

Cardiac has superhuman strength, speed and durability. He has a bulletproof skin, and his heart is powered by a beta-particle reactor. He wields a staff that projects beta-particle blasts.

— POWER RATING —

Intelligence	●●●●●●○○○○
Strength	●●●●○○○○○○
Speed	●●●○○○○○○○
Durability	●●●●○○○○○○
Energy Projection	●●●●○○○○○○
Fighting Skill	●●●●●○○○○○

CARLIE COOPER

A forensic detective with the New York City Police Department, Carlie Cooper is the childhood friend of Lily Hollister (alias Menace) and a former girlfriend of Peter Parker's. When Spider-Man was framed for murder, Carlie used her skills to clear his name.

One Tough Cop

Carlie is a reliable ally of Peter's and likes to unwind by skating with her roller derby team. Her detective skills are so strong that she managed to deduce Peter's secret identity as Spider-Man, temporarily driving a wedge between the two friends.

Carlie is an expert on Spider-Man's technology, including his web shooters and spider-tracers.

Peter and Carlie dated, but she felt betrayed after discovering the secrets Peter had kept from her for months.

Off-duty, Carlie keeps a close-knit circle of friends.

"Got a lead I want to follow. I know who's behind all this."

WEB FILE

Carlie does not possess any super powers, but she is a gifted forensic scientist and an expert in biology and technology.

— POWER RATING —

Intelligence	●●●●●●○○○○
Strength	●●○○○○○○○○
Speed	●●○○○○○○○○
Durability	●●●○○○○○○○
Energy Projection	●○○○○○○○○○
Fighting Skill	●●●○○○○○○○

CARNAGE

Crimson-coloured alien symbiote Carnage chose killer Cletus Kasady as its human host, resulting in a truly monstrous Super Villain. Carnage is so powerful that Spider-Man needs help from other heroes to defeat it. The symbiote has bonded with other hosts but always returns to Cletus to continue its mad rampage.

"I am the ultimate insanity! I am Carnage!"

WEB FILE

Carnage has superhuman strength, speed and durability. It can generate swing lines and vicious bladed weapons, and it can neutralize Spider-Man's spider-sense.

POWER RATING

Intelligence	●●●●●○○○○○
Strength	●●●●○○○○○○
Speed	●●●○○○○○○○
Durability	●●●●●●○○○○
Energy Projection	●●○○○○○○○○
Fighting Skill	●●●●●●○○○○

Relentless

Carnage is the most dangerous of all the alien symbiotes. It has no regard for human life and chose a relentless killer as its host. He is stronger than Spider-Man and its "parent" symbiote Venom combined. It craves chaos, destruction, and murder.

Symbiotic exterior can morph into different shapes.

Carnage has completely corrupted its human host.

Carnage uses its body's sharp tendrils as weapons to ensnare his enemies.

CARRION

Virus Effects

Carrion's abilities, including his eerie hovering and his deadly touch, appear supernatural in origin. But like most of Spider-Man's enemies, Carrion's powers are science-based and began in a laboratory.

The original Carrion was a clone of Professor Miles Warren, alias the Jackal. Transformed by a genetic virus into a pale-skinned monster, this Carrion died trying to kill Spider-Man. Later, Peter Parker's university classmate Malcolm McBride fell victim to the same virus. As the new Carrion, he joined forces with the villains Carnage, Shriek, and Hobgoblin to go on a rampage across New York.

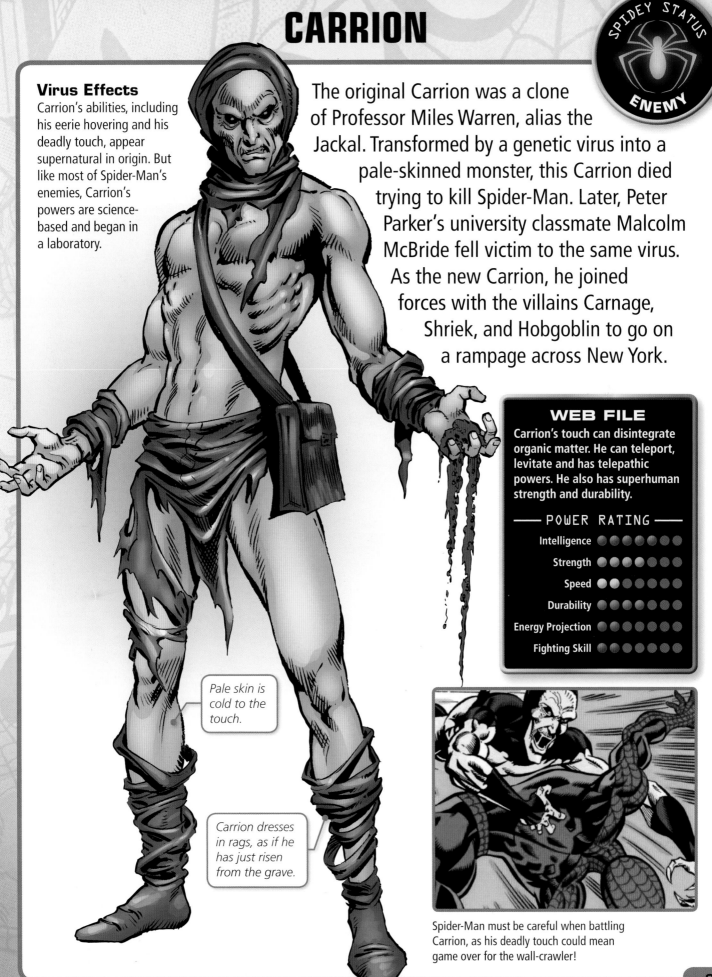

Pale skin is cold to the touch.

Carrion dresses in rags, as if he has just risen from the grave.

WEB FILE

Carrion's touch can disintegrate organic matter. He can teleport, levitate and has telepathic powers. He also has superhuman strength and durability.

— POWER RATING —

Intelligence	●●●●●●○○○○
Strength	●●●●●○○○○○
Speed	○●●○○○○○○○
Durability	●●●●●○○○○○
Energy Projection	●●●●○○○○○○
Fighting Skill	●●●●○○○○○○

Spider-Man must be careful when battling Carrion, as his deadly touch could mean game over for the wall-crawler!

23

CHAMELEON

Russian Dmitri Smerdyakov, alias the Chameleon, can copy anyone's appearance perfectly, and used his mimicry skills to become a spy for the Soviet Union. When Spider-Man foiled his plans, he became a criminal for hire. The Chameleon is the mastermind behind many of Spider-Man's trickiest cases.

A solid punch can interrupt the Chameleon's concentration and make him drop his disguise.

Chameleon's gadgets allow him to project holograms of his clothing.

An experimental serum makes his body completely malleable.

WEB FILE

Chameleon is a master of disguise and espionage, an explosives expert, and crack shot. His computer belt allows him to alter his appearance – including his clothing – at will.

── POWER RATING ──

Intelligence	●●●●●●●○
Strength	●●●○○○○○
Speed	●●○○○○○○
Durability	●●●○○○○○
Energy Projection	●○○○○○○○
Fighting Skill	●●●●○○○○

Family Ties

The Chameleon is related to the Kravinoff family, though he has no love for Kraven the Hunter or the other members of his clan. Nevertheless, he helped Kraven's wife Sasha Kravinoff organize the "Grim Hunt" that targeted Spider-Man and his friends for termination.

CHANGE

WEB FILE
Chance's armoured costume has wrist-blasters and ankle jets for flight, plus various other weapons and gadgets.

— POWER RATING —

Intelligence
Strength
Speed
Durability
Energy Projection
Fighting Skill

Bored with life as a professional gambler, Nicholas Powell became the mercenary Chance. Instead of charging a fee, Chance places a bet on his success – and pays his employer if he fails. Chance has learned that trying to kill Spider-Man is an expensive proposition!

"Bet you my share I kill both of 'em myself!"

Chance is willing to work with Super Heroes like Spider-Man, but he only really cares about himself.

Backpack contains power cells to charge his wrist-blasters.

Rolling the Dice
Chance sometimes teams up with the web-slinger to capture dangerous foes. One such team-up saw him and Spider-Man turn the tables on the villainous Life Foundation when they tried to double-cross Chance. Spider-Man is grateful for Chance's help but doesn't consider him a true hero.

Helmet allows 360-degree field of vision.

CHARLOTTE WITTER

Former fashion designer Charlotte Witter is the granddaughter of Madame Web and one of the few women to become Spider-Woman. When Doctor Octopus mutated her into a terrifying spider-hybrid, Charlotte absorbed the powers of every Spider-Woman who had come before her.

WEB FILE

Spider-Woman has superhuman strength and agility. She can fly, generate "venom blasts" and "psi-webs," and hypnotize others. Four spider legs extend from her back.

—— POWER RATING ——

Intelligence	●●●●○○○○○○
Strength	●●●●●○○○○○
Speed	●●●●○○○○○○
Durability	●●●○○○○○○○
Energy Projection	●●●●○○○○○○
Fighting Skill	●●●○○○○○○○

Charlotte can hypnotize men.

Out of Control

Possessing so much power affected Charlotte's mind, and she grew increasingly unhinged as her rampage continued. Spider-Man tried to stop her but she finally met defeat at the hands of the latest Spider-Woman, Mattie Franklin. Charlotte then changed back into her human form.

At the height of her power, Charlotte possessed every ability ever used by a spider-powered hero.

CLOAK AND DAGGER

Tyrone Johnson and Tandy Bowen are Cloak and Dagger, a mutant duo who are always prepared to help their friend Spider-Man. They first met as runaways, teaming up to fight New York's criminals. Since then they have become reliable allies of the Super Hero community.

The two heroes are dating and always look out for each other in times of trouble.

"We have come for you!"

Cloak can teleport himself and others, and also become ethereal.

Dagger uses telekenesis to control her light blades to direct them at her targets.

Forever a Team
Cloak and Dagger teamed up with Spider-Man to halt the New York City rampage by Carnage and his team of villains. For a time, it appeared that Carnage's ally Shriek had killed Dagger, driving Cloak to despair, but Dagger returned even more powerful than before.

WEB FILE
Cloak's body is a portal to the "Darkforce Dimension." He can teleport himself and others anywhere in the world, while Dagger can throw weapons of pure light.

— POWER RATING —
Intelligence	●●●●●○○○○○
Strength	●●●○○○○○○○
Speed	●●●◐○○○○○○
Durability	●●●●○○○○○○
Energy Projection	●●●●●●●○○○
Fighting Skill	●●●●●●○○○○

COLDHEART

Government operative Coldheart turned rogue following the death of her son. Armed with twin swords that could freeze any target, she set out to take revenge on Spider-Man and the Hobgoblin – the hero and villain she blamed for the tragedy in her past.

Coldheart's specialized gear is government issue, but it has been tailored for her unique set of skills.

"Coldheart is going on one last mission!"

Bulletproof armored costume.

Emotional Rescue

Coldheart's training as a special agent made her more than capable of defeating Spider-Man. Luckily for the wall-crawler, she had a change of heart after she encountered a young boy who reminded her of her own child. Showing mercy, Coldheart retreated.

Coldheart's quickness with a blade is a challenge for Spidey.

WEB FILE

Coldheart's body has cryokinetic power to create weapons of ice. Her icy blasts can shatter Spider-Man's webbing like glass. She is also a skilled martial artist and swordsman.

— POWER RATING —

Intelligence ●●●●●●○○○○
Strength ●●●●○○○○○○
Speed ●●○○○○○○○○
Durability ●●●●○○○○○○
Energy Projection ●●●●○○○○○○
Fighting Skill ●●●●●●○○○○

THE DAILY BUGLE

STAFF

Joe "Robbie" Robertson: Veteran reporter and newspaper editor.

Norah Winters: Investigative reporter who puts the story first.

Frederick Foswell: Reporter who lived a double life as Big Man.

Ben Urich: Hard-hitting journalist who battles corruption.

Phil Urich: Reporter who became the new Hobgoblin.

The Daily Bugle published negative headlines about Spider-Man for years on the orders of Editor-in-Chief J. Jonah Jameson – even while Peter Parker worked there as a photographer! Notable *Bugle* staffers have included editor Robbie Robertson and investigative reporter Ben Urich.

The Daily Bugle's newsroom is a busy hive of reporters, photographers, and editors.

Building a Legacy

When wealthy media magnate Dexter Bennett purchased the paper, he briefly renamed it *The DB* and focused on shallow celebrity gossip. *The Daily Bugle* now thrives under the leadership of Robbie Robertson, who has vowed to make *The Bugle* a world-class news operation both in print and online.

Spidey doesn't like the negative stories, but he's still a Bugle *fan.*

"The more I attack Spider-Man, the more people read my papers!"

29

DAREDEVIL

When an accident involving radioactive chemicals blinded Matt Murdoch, but boosted his remaining senses to superhuman levels, he became Daredevil, the man without fear! His father, a boxer, taught him how to fight, but Matt also studied law and defends the innocent as a trial lawyer.

Daredevil's identity as lawyer Matt Murdock is a well-kept secret, since few are aware of Daredevil's blindness.

Daredevil's trademarks include his horned mask and his "DD" insignia.

Watching From the Rooftops

Daredevil is the protector of Hell's Kitchen, a New York neighbourhood on the west side of Manhattan. He frequently crosses paths with Spider-Man during their nightly patrols of the city, and they often team up.

Daredevil's now-famous red outfit replaced his original yellow costume.

WEB FILE

Daredevil has superhuman senses. He can detect lies, and is a superb detective, tracker, and martial artist. His cane converts into a club and contains a cable and hook for crossing rooftops.

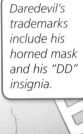

— POWER RATING —

Intelligence	●●●●●○○○○○
Strength	●●●●○○○○○○
Speed	●●○○○○○○○○
Durability	●●●○○○○○○○
Energy Projection	●○○○○○○○○○
Fighting Skill	●●●●●●●○○○

DARK AVENGERS

MEMBERS

1. **Iron Patriot:** Osborn wears a weaponized, armoured battlesuit capable of flight.

2. **Ares:** As the god of war, Ares is incredibly strong and one of the best fighters in existence.

3. **Bullseye (as Hawkeye):** Can throw or shoot any projectile with perfect accuracy.

4. **Moonstone (as Ms. Marvel):** Has the powers of flight, intangibility, and shooting photon blasts.

5. **Daken (as Wolverine):** Has mutant healing factor and retractable metal claws.

6. **Sentry:** Possesses limitless powers of strength, speed and molecular control.

Norman Osborn used his political power to create a new team of Avengers under his personal control. Calling himself the Iron Patriot, Osborn recruited the Sentry and other villains to his team, including several hired to impersonate Ms. Marvel, Wolverine, and Spider-Man. Together, they became the Dark Avengers.

Osborn's Downfall

Norman Osborn changed the line-up of his Dark Avengers over time. Eventually, he used his team to attack Thor's people during the Siege of Asgard. In the aftermath, Osborn was arrested and the original team of Dark Avengers disbanded.

DEADPOOL

Known as "the Merc with a Mouth," Deadpool is a high-energy jokester. A survivor of the same Weapon X facility that created Wolverine, Deadpool is sometimes a friend to Spider-Man. However, the only person who truly understands Deadpool is Deadpool himself.

WEB FILE

Deadpool has superhuman strength, stamina, agility and speed. He also has a superhuman healing factor, and extended longevity. He is an expert martial artist and skilled linguist.

— POWER RATING —

Intelligence	●●●●●○○○○○
Strength	●●●●●●●○○○
Speed	●●○○○○○○○○
Durability	●●●●●●○○○○
Energy Projection	●●●○○○○○○○
Fighting Skill	●●●●●●●●○○

Ammunition and grenades are in belt pouches.

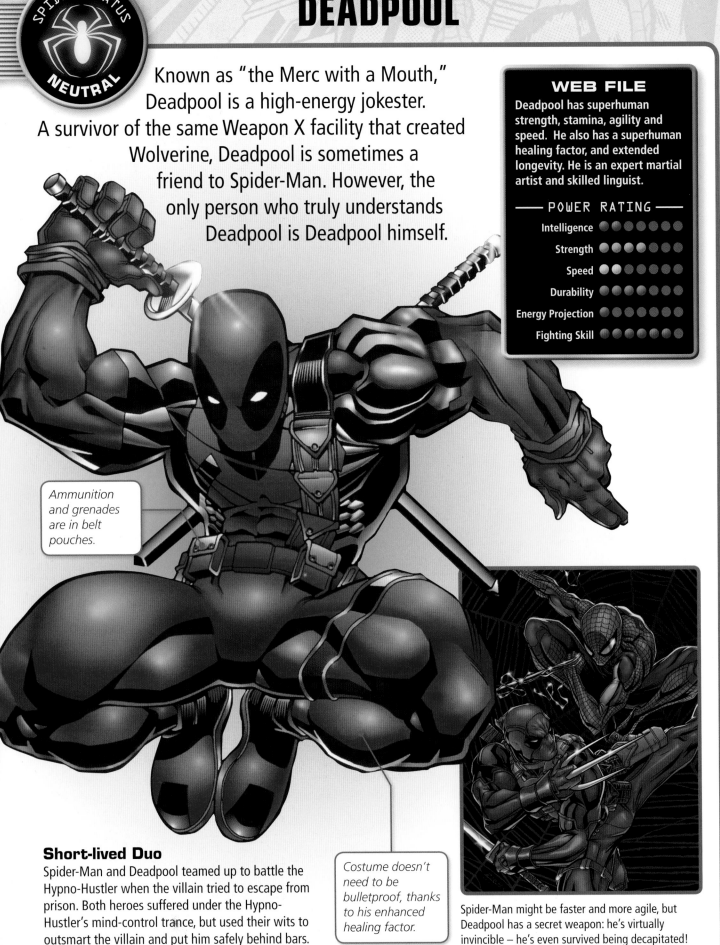

Costume doesn't need to be bulletproof, thanks to his enhanced healing factor.

Short-lived Duo

Spider-Man and Deadpool teamed up to battle the Hypno-Hustler when the villain tried to escape from prison. Both heroes suffered under the Hypno-Hustler's mind-control trance, but used their wits to outsmart the villain and put him safely behind bars.

Spider-Man might be faster and more agile, but Deadpool has a secret weapon: he's virtually invincible – he's even survived being decapitated!

DEBRA WHITMAN

Tormented by her thoughts about Spider-Man and her painful past, Debra sought professional help.

Debra Whitman met Peter Parker when she was a secretary at Empire State University's biophysics department. The two soon started a romance. But when Debra began hallucinating that Peter was actually Spider-Man, her visions came dangerously close to the truth.

"Either Peter Parker is Spider-Man, or I am hopelessly insane!"

A Better Life

Debra had other problems besides her obsession with Spider-Man, including a cruel husband who had forced her to seek a separation and a complicated life at ESU. Peter eventually wore the Spider-Man costume for Debra as part of her therapy, and the experience gave her the confidence to ask for a divorce.

Debra avoided conflict and tried not to draw attention to herself.

WEB FILE

Debra lacks super powers or combat training, but she is a skilled administrative aide and writer.

— POWER RATING —

Intelligence	●●●●●○○○○
Strength	●●●○○○○○○
Speed	●●○○○○○○○
Durability	●●●○○○○○○
Energy Projection	●○○○○○○○○
Fighting Skill	●●●○○○○○○

DEMOGOBLIN

When the Hobgoblin traded his soul for more power, a demon was bonded to him. Its supernatural abilities helped him to fight Spider-Man and Moon Knight, but the demon soon separated from its human host, and the Demogoblin was born!

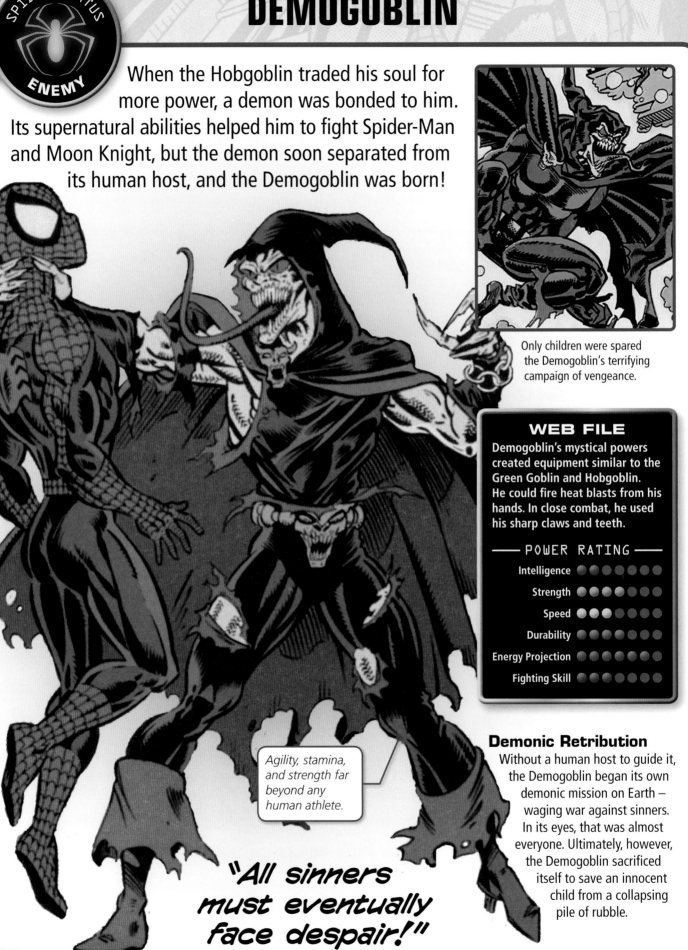

Only children were spared the Demogoblin's terrifying campaign of vengeance.

WEB FILE

Demogoblin's mystical powers created equipment similar to the Green Goblin and Hobgoblin. He could fire heat blasts from his hands. In close combat, he used his sharp claws and teeth.

— POWER RATING —

Intelligence	●●●●●○○○○○
Strength	●●●●●●○○○○
Speed	●●●○○○○○○○
Durability	●●●●●○○○○○
Energy Projection	●●●●○○○○○○
Fighting Skill	●●●●○○○○○○

Agility, stamina, and strength far beyond any human athlete.

Demonic Retribution
Without a human host to guide it, the Demogoblin began its own demonic mission on Earth — waging war against sinners. In its eyes, that was almost everyone. Ultimately, however, the Demogoblin sacrificed itself to save an innocent child from a collapsing pile of rubble.

"All sinners must eventually face despair!"

DOCTOR DOOM

WEB FILE

Doom is both a scientific genius and sorceror. He can transfer his consciousness into another person. His battlesuit contains advanced weaponry and increases his physical abilities.

── POWER RATING ──

Intelligence	●●●●●●●○○○
Strength	●●●●○○○○○○
Speed	●●○○○○○○○○
Durability	●●●●●○○○○○
Energy Projection	●●●●●○○○○○
Fighting Skill	●●●●○○○○○○

Doctor Doom's armour is made from titanium and uses nuclear energy to power its weapons systems.

The supreme leader of Latveria, Doctor Doom schemes to conquer the world from behind an iron mask. He blames the Fantastic Four's Reed Richards for the accident that scarred his face, and uses his genius-level intellect to seek revenge on him and his allies, including Spider-Man.

Doom versus Spidey

In one of Spider-Man's earliest adventures, Doctor Doom tried to trick the wall-crawler into bringing down the Fantastic Four. His plan failed, so Doctor Doom tried to destroy Spider-Man instead. In a case of mistaken identity, Doom nearly killed Peter's high school classmate Flash Thompson.

"You are not fighting one of your usual, insipid antagonists now, Spider-Man!"

Doctor Doom does respect his foes. He considers Spider-Man one of his most worthy adversaries, though he can be angered by the wall-crawler's wisecracks.

DOCTOR OCTOPUS

With four cybernetic arms and a brilliant brain, Dr. Otto Octavius has earned his title as the arch-enemy of Spider-Man. Doc Ock has tangled with Spider-Man in many different ways, from his creation of the Sinister Six to his romantic courtship of Peter Parker's Aunt May.

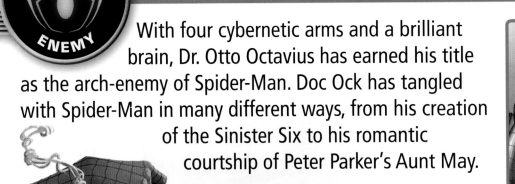

His mechanical tentacles give Doctor Octopus the mobility and strength he would otherwise lack.

Doc Ock's greatest weapon is his criminal intellect.

Starting From Scratch
When Doc Ock realized he had only months to live, he transferred his mind into Peter's body and started a new career as the "Superior" Spider-Man! But Peter's memories also showed Otto how to become a true hero.

WEB FILE
Scientific genius Doc Ock controls his four electrically powered tentacles with his mind. They can operate independently and are equipped with hugely powerful pincers.

— POWER RATING —
Intelligence	●●●●●●●○○○
Strength	●●●●●○○○○○
Speed	●●●○○○○○○○
Durability	●●●●○○○○○○
Energy Projection	●●○○○○○○○○
Fighting Skill	●●●●○○○○○○

Not particularly agile, Doc Ock uses his tentacles for fighting.

DOCTOR STRANGE

WEB FILE

The greatest magician on Earth, Doctor Strange can project his body on the astral plane, and communicate telepathically. His cloak of levitation enables him to fly.

—— POWER RATING ——

Intelligence	●●●●●●○○○○
Strength	●●○○○○○○○○
Speed	●◐○○○○○○○○
Durability	●●●○○○○○○○
Energy Projection	●●●●●●●○○○
Fighting Skill	●●●●●○○○○○

Dr. Stephen Strange lost his ability to perform surgery after a car accident, but learned the mystic arts to become Earth's Sorcerer Supreme. Doctor Strange teamed up with the web-slinger to defeat Baron Mordo. He's been one of Spider-Man's closest advisors ever since.

Expert in the Occult

Even when he's not home, Doctor Strange is happy to appear in spirit form to answer questions whenever Peter Parker comes to call. Despite his immense skill with sorcery, Doctor Strange is the first to admit that even magic has its limits.

"By the all-seeing Eye of Agamotto!"

When out among the public, Doctor Strange tries to blend in.

Mystical artifacts are concealed beneath trenchcoat.

As Spider-Man has a scientific background, Doctor Strange is a valuable ally when Spidey has to enter the realm of magic and sorcery.

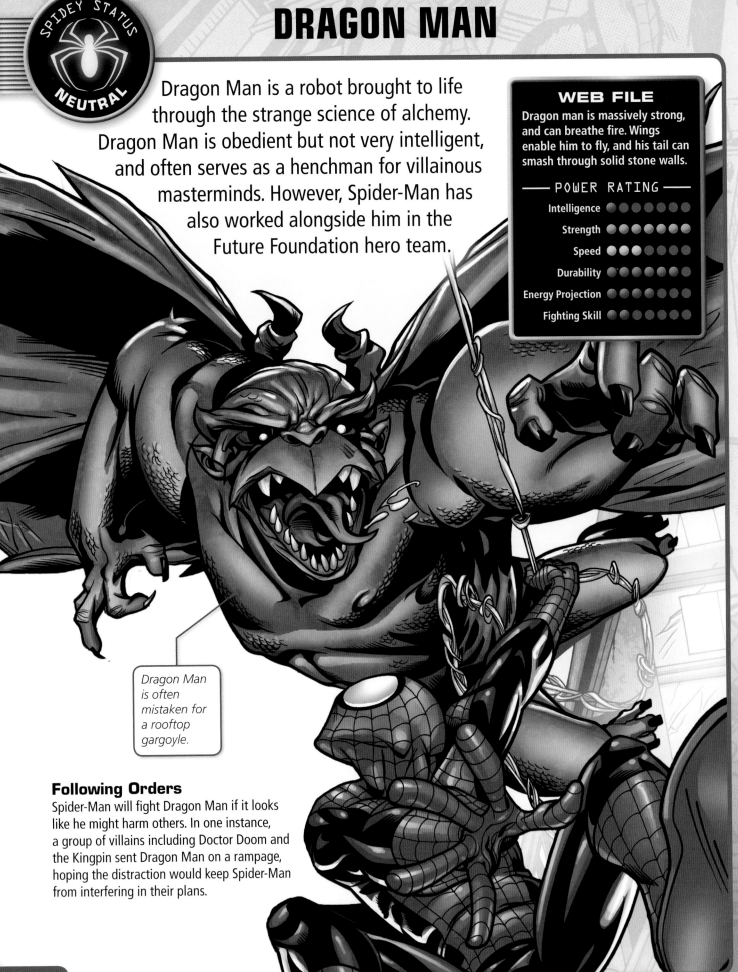

DRAGON MAN

Dragon Man is a robot brought to life through the strange science of alchemy. Dragon Man is obedient but not very intelligent, and often serves as a henchman for villainous masterminds. However, Spider-Man has also worked alongside him in the Future Foundation hero team.

WEB FILE

Dragon man is massively strong, and can breathe fire. Wings enable him to fly, and his tail can smash through solid stone walls.

POWER RATING

Intelligence	●○○○○○○
Strength	●●●●○○○
Speed	●●●○○○○
Durability	●●●○○○○
Energy Projection	●○○○○○○
Fighting Skill	●●●○○○○

Dragon Man is often mistaken for a rooftop gargoyle.

Following Orders

Spider-Man will fight Dragon Man if it looks like he might harm others. In one instance, a group of villains including Doctor Doom and the Kingpin sent Dragon Man on a rampage, hoping the distraction would keep Spider-Man from interfering in their plans.

EL MUERTO

WEB FILE

El Muerto is a highly skilled wrestler, and his mask gives him superhuman strength and stamina.

POWER RATING

Intelligence	●●●●●●●●
Strength	●●●●●●●●
Speed	●●●●●●●●●
Durability	●●●●●●●●
Energy Projection	●●●●●●●●
Fighting Skill	●●●●●●●●

The magical Mask of El Muerto has been in the Estrada family for generations. Each challenger has to wrestle and defeat the mask's former wearer. Juan-Carlos, the current El Muerto, came to New York to wrestle Spider-Man. During the match, Spidey accidentally injured El Muerto with a stinger that sprang from his wrist, briefly paralyzing him.

El Muerto is superhumanly strong, but not as strong as Spidey.

"It doesn't matter why you lose, so long as you do."

The Power of Two

After El Muerto recovered from the injuries he had sustained in the wrestling match, he teamed up with Spider-Man to fight the Mexican god El Dorado. Disappointed by El Muerto's failure in the ring against Spider-Man, El Dorado tried to kill him, but couldn't overcome both heroes.

Spider-Man let El Muerto get the upper hand at first, but never meant to injure him.

ELECTRO

While working as a power-service lineman, Maxwell Dillon gained electrical powers in an accident. He decided to turn to crime as Electro. One of the first Super Villains to go up against Spider-Man, Electro was a founding member of the Sinister Six, and is one of Spidey's most frequent foes.

"The world will once again know the terrible power of Electro!"

Spidey's super-strength gives him some resistance to injury, but he has no defence against electric shock.

Electro's costume helps absorb damage.

Any contact with Electro could mean a fatal jolt.

Charged Up
Over time, Electro's powers have increased, and he can now black out the entire New York City power grid. He boosts his powers by drawing energy from electrical equipment, but risks being short-circuited by water.

Electrical bolts burst from hands.

WEB FILE
Electro can shape electricity into whips, tendrils and nets. He can also fire electric bolts, travel along power lines and control electronic machinery.

— POWER RATING —
Intelligence	●●●○○○○○○○
Strength	●●○○○○○○○○
Speed	●●○○○○○○○○
Durability	●●●○○○○○○○
Energy Projection	●●●●●●○○○○
Fighting Skill	●●●○○○○○○○

ENFORCERS

MEMBERS

1. **Ox:** Tough brawler with big muscles.

2. **Montana:** Good with a lariat and able to ensnare any foe.

3. **Fancy Dan:** A judo and karate expert who can dodge most blows.

The Enforcers work as hired muscle in New York's organized crime scene, answering to bosses like the Big Man, the Green Goblin, and the Kingpin. On one of their first assignments, the Enforcers lost badly when they clashed with Spider-Man. Since then they have repeatedly tried to eliminate the wall-crawler.

Ox is hugely strong but not overly bright.

"Spider-Man? You ain't about to spoil our fun!"

Tough Guys

When crime boss the Big Man hired the Enforcers to extort money from Betty Brant, Spider-Man soon swung in to protect her. The wall-crawler let himself be captured and taken to the Enforcers' hideout. He defeated the thugs and turned them over to the police.

When the Enforcers targeted Spider-Man at an amusement park, Spidey found his escape hampered by Montana's skill with a lariat.

Fancy Dan is a crack shot with most firearms.

EZEKIEL

The mysterious Ezekiel claimed that Spider-Man's powers were not caused by a radioactive spider bite, but were bestowed on him by the mystical totems of animal spirits. Ezekiel possessed spider-powers too, but he used his to become a wealthy corporate executive.

Ezekiel usually dresses in a business suit, but goes barefoot for better contact when climbing walls.

He may be old, but Ezekiel is kept strong through his spider-powers.

Guidance of an Expert

After learning Spider-Man's identity, he told Peter Parker that he could help him achieve his destiny as the bearer of the spider totem. Together, the two defeated the ageless Morlun, a monster who fed on the life-force of the totem.

Like Spider-Man, Ezekiel can crawl up walls.

WEB FILE

Ezekiel's abilities are similar to Spider-Man's. His "spider-sense" warns him of danger and he can cling to most surfaces.

— POWER RATING —

Intelligence	●●●●●○○
Strength	●●●●●○○
Speed	●●●○○○○
Durability	●●●●○○○
Energy Projection	●●○○○○○
Fighting Skill	●●●●○○○

FANTASTIC FOUR

The Fantastic Four are more like a family than a Super Hero team. They received super powers in an outer-space accident and, as Mister Fantastic, the Invisible Woman, the Human Torch, and the Thing, fought evil from their HQ, the Baxter Building. Spidey joined when the team became known as the Future Foundation.

Spider-Man has travelled with the Fantastic Four to the past, the future, and alternate dimensions. He is close friends with its four teammates.

Mr. Fantastic can stretch to unbelievable lengths.

Planetary Defenders
The Fantastic Four are always at the front line when cosmic events threaten the Earth, whether it's an invasion from the Negative Zone or the arrival of an omnipotent alien Super Villain.

The Human Torch is one of Spidey's closest friends.

MEMBERS

1. **The Thing:** Super-strong and nearly indestructible in his rocky body.

2. **Mr. Fantastic:** Genius scientist who can stretch his body to incredible lengths.

3. **The Invisible Woman:** Able to turn invisible and project unbreakable force fields.

4. **The Human Torch:** Able to fly, cover his body in flames and hurl firebolts.

FIRESTAR

Angelica Jones is a mutant who can control microwave radiation. Friendly and outgoing, she has long been an ally of Spider-Man's, teaming up with him and Iceman of the X-Men for a brief time. Firestar is very much a team player and has worked with the New Warriors and the Avengers.

WEB FILE

Firestar has the mutant ability to project microwave energy and generate intense heat. Her microwave energies also enable her to fly.

— POWER RATING —

Intelligence	●●●●●○○
Strength	●●○○○○○
Speed	●●●○○○○
Durability	●●●●○○○
Energy Projection	●●●●●●○
Fighting Skill	●●●●○○○

Fire blasts are projected from hands.

Firestar is surrounded by a flaming aura when in flight.

Amazing Friend

Firestar often pops up when Spider-Man needs assistance. Her positive attitude makes her an indispensable teammate with a knack of appearing in the right place at the right time. Active as a hero since the age of thirteen, Firestar is growing more powerful with every year.

"Boy am I glad to see you! We can really use the help!"

Firestar's costume is immune to her heat powers.

Firestar treats her Super Hero teammates like family, and is fiercely loyal to those that she trusts.

FLASH THOMPSON

Flash served several tours of duty in the U.S. Army and won recognition for his bravery.

Football star Flash Thompson was the most popular student at Midtown High School, but used to bully Peter Parker. After Peter became Spider-Man, the two became friends. Flash lost his legs serving with the U.S. Army but, thanks to a government experiment, regained his mobility by becoming the new host for the Venom symbiote.

"I don't need a medal to remind me to do the right thing."

Flash considers himself Spider-Man's number one fan.

Beneath his cocky exterior Flash has the heart of a hero.

Growing Up

As a teenager, Flash admired Spider-Man but hated "puny" Peter Parker. He later became a hero in his own right as a military-sanctioned operative armed with the powers of Venom.

WEB FILE

As the host for Venom, Flash has powers similar to Spider-Man, with superhuman strength, speed and agility, wall-crawling and the ability to shoot a web-like substance.

— POWER RATING —

Intelligence	●●●○○○○
Strength	●●●●○○○
Speed	●●○○○○○
Durability	●●●○○○○
Energy Projection	●○○○○○○
Fighting Skill	●●●●○○○

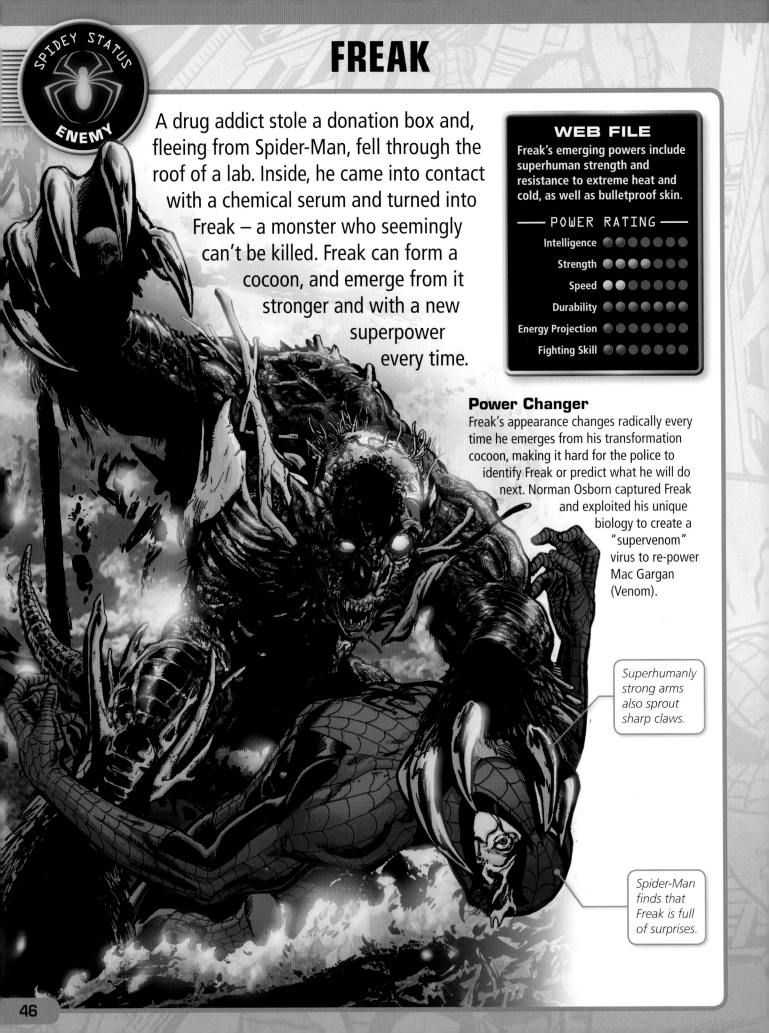

FREAK

A drug addict stole a donation box and, fleeing from Spider-Man, fell through the roof of a lab. Inside, he came into contact with a chemical serum and turned into Freak – a monster who seemingly can't be killed. Freak can form a cocoon, and emerge from it stronger and with a new superpower every time.

WEB FILE

Freak's emerging powers include superhuman strength and resistance to extreme heat and cold, as well as bulletproof skin.

—— POWER RATING ——

Intelligence	●●●●●●●●
Strength	●●●●●●●●
Speed	●●●●●●●●
Durability	●●●●●●●●
Energy Projection	●●●●●●●●
Fighting Skill	●●●●●●●●

Power Changer

Freak's appearance changes radically every time he emerges from his transformation cocoon, making it hard for the police to identify Freak or predict what he will do next. Norman Osborn captured Freak and exploited his unique biology to create a "supervenom" virus to re-power Mac Gargan (Venom).

Superhumanly strong arms also sprout sharp claws.

Spider-Man finds that Freak is full of surprises.

FRIGHTFUL FOUR

MEMBERS

1. **Wizard:** Scientific genius whose powered armour enables him to fly and to fire energy blasts.

2. **Hydro-Man:** Able to turn any part of his body into a water-like substance and back again.

3. **Trapster:** Outfitted with a variety of traps and glue-shooters.

4. **Salamandra:** Can teleport and transform into a dragon, produce blasts of energy and teleport.

The Frightful Four set out to be a villainous version of the Fantastic Four. The team's lineup often changes, but evil genius the Wizard remains the leader. After many defeats by Super Heroes such as the Fantastic Four and Spider-Man, the team longs to come out on top.

Salamandra has martial arts training.

"Spider-Man is no longer a threat to the Frightful Four!"

Wizard's battlesuit generates force field.

Four for Fighting

One grouping of the Frightful Four decided that the best way to take down the Fantastic Four was by targeting Spider-Man! Trapster posed as the wall-crawler to sneak inside the Fantastic Four's headquarters, but the real Spider-Man helped stop the imposter and his teammates.

Hydro-Man can make his fists hard as ice.

Trapster's adhesive boots and gloves enable him to walk up walls.

FUSION

People are amazed when they see Fusion wielding the incredible powers of Thor or the Thing, but it isn't real. Fusion is merely spinning illusions. He first used his powers of persuasion to get rich, but after his son died trying to imitate Spider-Man, Fusion launched a cruel vendetta against the web-slinger.

WEB FILE
Fusion's uncanny powers of persuasion can make people perceive and believe whatever he wants them to.

— POWER RATING —
Intelligence ●●●●●●●
Strength ●●●
Speed ●●
Durability ●●●●
Energy Projection ●●●●●
Fighting Skill ●●●●●

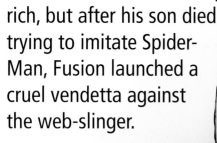

Fusion usually wears a black and gold suit, but he can alter it at will.

> "I am Fusion, an amalgam of every hero and criminal in this city."

Weapons are mostly for show.

Every Power Under the Sun
Fusion burst onto the scene when he tried to rob a New York City bank, attracting the attention of Spider-Man. The illusions conjured up by Fusion included Captain America's shield, Wolverine's claws, and the mechanical tentacles of Doctor Octopus.

Fusion only appears to possess the weapons of Spider-Man's foes, but when he teamed up with Doc Ock the tentacles were for real!

GAUNT

Mendel Stromm provided the brainpower during Oscorp Industries' early years, but was sent to prison by his partner, Norman Osborn, for stealing company funds. Thirsting for revenge, Mendel decided to use robot technology to get back at Osborn. Ultimately, he transferred his brainwaves into a mechanical body, emerging as Gaunt, a deadly cyborg who threatened both Norman Osborn and Spider-Man.

Gaunt's hidden weapons systems, such as arm cannons, blades, and grenades, can leave Spidey at a severe disadvantage.

Mechanical systems include weapons and life support.

Cybernetic parts have extended Mendel Stromm's life.

"Give up, and I'll make it quick!"

WEB FILE

Stromm is a scientific genius who specializes in inventing robots, which he uses as weapons. As Gaunt, he has superhuman strength and durability.

— POWER RATING —

Intelligence	●●●●●●○○○○
Strength	●●●●●○○○○○
Speed	●●○○○○○○○○
Durability	●●●●●○○○○○
Energy Projection	●●●●○○○○○○
Fighting Skill	●●●●●●○○○○

Machine Man

Stromm had made an earlier attempt at transferring his brainwaves into a mechanical frame, assuming the identity of Robot Master. Spidey made short work of that monster. Now, as Gaunt, Stromm's body is composed of both living tissue and robotic components.

GEORGE STACY

Captain George Stacy of the N.Y.P.D. was one of Spider-Man's most reliable supporters. He was a friend to Peter Parker too, having secretly discovered the truth about Peter's double identity. A hero to the end, he died while saving a child's life during a battle between Spider-Man and Doctor Octopus.

WEB FILE

Stacy was an excellent detective and leader, trained in hand-to-hand combat techniques and the use of firearms.

— POWER RATING —

Intelligence	●●●●●●●
Strength	●●●●●●
Speed	●●●●●●
Durability	●●●●●●
Energy Projection	●●●●●●
Fighting Skill	●●●●●●

Capt. Stacy projected an air of quiet competence.

A Good Man

His sharp powers of observation allowed Captain Stacy to determine that Peter Parker wore Spider-Man's mask, but he kept the secret and only revealed it to Peter during his dying moments. His daughter Gwen blamed the death of her father on Spider-Man.

"Be good to her son! She loves you so very much!"

A lifetime on the police force left Capt. Stacy reliant on a cane.

Spider-Man felt guilty for the events that led up to Captain Stacy's death and vowed to do better.

GHOST RIDER

The Spirit of Vengeance rides a motorcycle! Johnny Blaze and Danny Ketch have both served as the bonded human partners of an unforgiving demon, becoming the flame-headed apparition Ghost Rider. Because Spider-Man is a science expert, Ghost Rider is a helpful ally when he faces supernatural threats.

Ghost Rider's magical powers can be unpredictable, keeping Spidey guessing.

Ghost Rider's chain can be used as a whip.

Devilish Bargain
The infernal powers wielded by Ghost Rider come from the demon Zarathos, a rival of Mephisto's in the spiritual underworld. Ghost Rider's human hosts must constantly struggle to stay in control, and take inspiration from heroes like Spider-Man.

Motorcycle leaves a fiery trail wherever it goes.

WEB FILE
Ghost Rider's mystical motorcycle can drive up walls and he carries a heavy chain as a weapon. He also has superhuman strength and durability.

— POWER RATING —
Intelligence ●●●●●○○○○○
Strength ●●●●●●○○○○
Speed ●●○○○○○○○○
Durability ●●●●●●●○○○
Energy Projection ●●●●●●○○○○
Fighting Skill ●●●●○○○○○○

GIBBON

No one takes the Gibbon seriously as a hero or a villain – not even Spider-Man! Despite remarkable super-ape abilities, nothing ever seems to go the Gibbon's way. Looking for safety in numbers, the Gibbon once teamed up with fellow luckless crooks Spot, Grizzly and Kangaroo as the Spider-Man Revenge Squad.

WEB FILE

The Gibbon has the mutant power of incredible, ape-like agility, enhanced by a secret formula given to him by Kraven the Hunter.

— POWER RATING —

Intelligence	●●●○○○○○○○
Strength	●●●●○○○○○○
Speed	●●○○○○○○○○
Durability	●●●○○○○○○○
Energy Projection	●○○○○○○○○○
Fighting Skill	●●●○○○○○○○

Hapless Hero

The Gibbon later tried to become a hero, and started a new partnership with Grizzly. They obtained a special car to drive during their missions, but they lost it when the Gibbon forgot that it couldn't be driven under water..

"This smoke from the blast is murder on my asthma!"

Gibbon is as agile as Spider-Man, but doesn't always think before he acts.

Gibbon's shaggy fur gives him an extra layer of protection.

Gibbon has a habit of getting in over his head, requiring Spider-Man to swing to the rescue.

GLORY GRANT

Glory Grant was working as a model when she moved into Peter Parker's apartment building. The two became friends, and Peter helped her land a job at *The Daily Bugle* as J. Jonah Jameson's secretary. Glory handled her boss's demands with ease, but fell out with Spider-Man when she fell in love with one of the villainous Lobo Brothers.

J. Jonah Jameson respects Glory though he rarely admits it.

WEB FILE

Glory has excellent administrative, computer, and secretarial skills, and is also an experienced scuba diver.

— POWER RATING —

Intelligence	●●●○○○○
Strength	●●○○○○○
Speed	●○○○○○○
Durability	●○○○○○○
Energy Projection	●○○○○○○
Fighting Skill	●●○○○○○

Upward Mobility

After J. Jonah Jameson was elected mayor of New York City, Glory Grant signed on as his personal aide. In her new role, Glory is responsible for handling her boss's schedule and maintaining a friendly relationship with the press, including the reporters of *The Daily Bugle*.

Glory has pursued careers in modelling and administration.

"You're a photographer and I'm a model. Fate has thrown us together."

As Peter Parker's new neighbour, Glory appreciated his photography expertise. She soon landed a job at *The Daily Bugle*.

GOG

Reptilian alien Gog was just a baby when the spacecraft he was travelling in crashed in the dinosaur-infested jungles of the Savage Land. Kraven the Hunter found Gog and raised him to become his partner in a scheme to wrest control of the Savage Land from its protector, Ka-Zar. Spider-Man helped Ka-Zar to send both villains packing.

Spider-Man is really made to feel small by the gargantuan Gog whenever the two opponents battle.

Stranger in a Strange Land

Gog is unable to speak any Earth languages. He can only make animal-like noises and form incomprehensible, alien words. Nevertheless, he is highly intelligent, able to operate futuristic technology and understand the commands of Kraven the Hunter and the other allies he has found on this strange new planet.

Gog is intelligent but easily led by villains to serve their evil ends.

Outfit worn by Gog's space-going native species.

WEB FILE

Gog is massively tall and heavy, super-strong and super-durable. He wears bracelets that enable him to teleport.

— POWER RATING —

Intelligence	●●●●●●○
Strength	●●●●●●●
Speed	●●○○○○○
Durability	●●●●●●○
Energy Projection	●●○○○○○
Fighting Skill	●●●●●○○

GRAY GOBLIN

When angry, mentally unstable Gabriel Stacy attacked Spider-Man. The wall-crawler was reluctant to fight back for fear of hurting him.

Norman Osborn's twin children, Sarah and Gabriel, believed Peter Parker was their father. Osborn told them that Peter rejected them after their mother, Gwen Stacy, died. When Gabriel discovered that Osborn was their father, he blamed Spider-Man for Gwen's death; he donned a version of the Green Goblin suit to become the Gray Goblin and attack Spidey.

A Life Built on Lies
Gabriel injected himself with strength-enhancing Green Goblin serum and used the Gray Goblin identity to lash out at Spider-Man. Sarah halted a potentially fatal clash by shooting Gabriel's glider from under him. After crashing to earth, Gabriel was left with no memory of his brief Gray Goblin career.

Costume taken from one of the Green Goblin's secret weapons caches.

WEB FILE
The Goblin formula halts the rapid aging caused by Gabriel's Goblin blood. It also gives him superhuman strength, durability and reflexes, and enhances his healing factor and intelligence.

— POWER RATING —
Intelligence ●●●●●○○○
Strength ●●●●○○○○
Speed ●●○○○○○○
Durability ●●●○○○○○
Energy Projection ●●●○○○○○
Fighting Skill ●●●●○○○○

GREEN GOBLIN NORMAN OSBORN

A smoke-spewing glider and a crazed cackle are the Green Goblin's trademarks. In a quest for power, businessman Norman Osborn invented a serum that gave him incredible strength but cost him his sanity. As the Green Goblin, he terrorized the city during Spider-Man's early career.

The Death of Gwen Stacy

The Green Goblin's most notorious crime was to throw Peter Parker's girlfriend, Gwen Stacy, from the top of a bridge. The Green Goblin seemingly died while fighting Spider-Man when his own goblin glider crashed into him. But this would not be the last that the world would hear of Norman Osborn.

WEB FILE

The Goblin formula gives Osborn superhuman physical abilities. His throwing weapons include pumpkin gas/smoke/explosive bombs. His tough Goblin armour includes gloves that fire electrical bolts.

POWER RATING

Intelligence ●●●●●○○
Strength ●●●●○○○
Speed ●●●○○○○
Durability ●●●●○○○
Energy Projection ●●●○○○○
Fighting Skill ●●●●○○○

Gas grenades kept within close reach.

Super-strength punches can stun Spidey.

"Spider-Man is my enemy! My mortal foe!"

The Goblin Glider can hover in place or reach jet-powered speeds. It responds to remote control.

GREEN GOBLIN HARRY OSBORN

WEB FILE

Harry has superhuman abilities thanks to his father's Green Goblin serum; he uses Goblin equipment, including pumpkin bombs, razor-sharp bats, power-emitting gloves and glider.

POWER RATING

Intelligence ●●●●●●○○○○
Strength ●●●●●○○○○○
Speed ●●●○○○○○○○
Durability ●●●●○○○○○○
Energy Projection ●●●●○○○○○○
Fighting Skill ●●●○○○○○○○

Harry was devastated when he discovered that his father, Norman, was the villainous Green Goblin and had died battling Spider-Man. Harry then found out that Spider-Man was his best friend, Peter Parker! Crazy with grief, Harry suited up as a second Green Goblin to get revenge.

"Now at last, the time has come for the Green Goblin to live again!"

Missing in Action

Exposure to his father's strength serum gave Harry incredible abilities, but the serum slowly began to poison him. To recover, Harry dropped out of sight for years, and many believed him dead. However, he eventually returned from a long spell in rehab and became friends with Peter once again.

Harry's body reacted badly to the Green Goblin serum.

Harry both loves and hates his father – and the Green Goblin.

The Goblin's smoke bombs sometimes included mind-altering gasses, giving the villain a sneaky edge over Spider-Man.

GRIM HUNTER

Vladimir Kravinoff blamed Spider-Man for the death of his father, Kraven the Hunter. Inspired by a hero from an ancestral legend, he became the Grim Hunter – and made Spidey his prey! By studying Kraven's journals, Vladimir learned all Spider-Man's fighting moves.

Unlike Kraven, the Grim Hunter wears protective armour.

His Father's Footsteps

The Grim Hunter pursued both Spider-Man and his clone Ben Reilly (the Scarlet Spider) in his quest to restore his family's honor. He was killed by Kaine, another clone of Spider-Man, but returned to life through a mystic ritual, this time as a human-lion hybrid.

"Excellent reflexes. But I will not miss twice."

Body is super strong due to his father's mystical serum.

A ritual performed by his mother, Sasha, restored Vladimir Kravinoff to life as a lion-like predator, hungry for a piece of Spider-Man's hide.

WEB FILE

The Grim Hunter has superhuman physical abilities and fighting skills. He wears armour on his arms and torso, his gauntlets fire electrical shocks, and he has wrist dart launchers.

— POWER RATING —

Intelligence	●●●●●●○○
Strength	●●●●●●●○
Speed	●●●●○○○○
Durability	●●●●●○○○
Energy Projection	●●●○○○○○
Fighting Skill	●●●●●●●○

GRIZZLY

WEB FILE

Grizzly's suit gives him superhuman strength and durability and his fangs and claws can tear steel. He is also a skilled wrestler.

— POWER RATING —

Intelligence ●●●○○○○○○○
Strength ●●●●●○○○○○
Speed ●●○○○○○○○○
Durability ●●●●○○○○○○
Energy Projection ○○○○○○○○○○
Fighting Skill ●●●●●○○○○○

Maxwell Markham was a famous pro wrestler until an article in *The Daily Bugle* exposed him as a bully. Wearing a strength-enhancing exosuit given to him by the Jackal, he showed up at *The DB* looking for payback as Grizzly. After repeatedly losing to Spidey, Grizzly teamed up with other villains, with little success. He has even tried becoming a hero!

Bear head does not restrict his vision.

"A spider ain't no match for a bear!"

Barely Making It

Grizzly entered into a partnership with the enthusiastic Gibbon, but their efforts have always ended in failure. The truth is, Grizzly values fame and fortune more than friendship. To make matters worse, his short temper makes him suddenly lash out – even at his own teammates.

Grizzly has sought to reinvent himself numerous times, but he has found it very difficult to escape the shadow of his criminal past.

Dangerous claws on hands and feet.

GWEN STACY

Gwen Stacy was Peter Parker's first love and Spider-Man's greatest loss. Gwen and Peter began dating when they were students at Empire State University. But when the Green Goblin kidnapped Gwen and threw her from a bridge, Spider-Man wasn't able to save her.

Gwen died of her injuries before Spider-Man could get her to a hospital.

Spider-Man would always feel guilty for not preventing the tragic fates that befell Gwen and her father.

Lost Love

When Gwen's father, Captain George Stacy, died during a battle between Spider-Man and Doctor Octopus, Gwen blamed the web-swinger for the tragedy. Peter wanted to tell Gwen the truth, but she died before Peter could reveal his identity to the woman he loved.

"I'm so mixed up! If only Peter were here."

WEB FILE

Gwen was a gifted biochemistry student and a curious, quick thinker. She was well-liked for her friendliness and generosity.

POWER RATING

Intelligence	●●●●●○○
Strength	●●○○○○○
Speed	●●○○○○○
Durability	●●○○○○○
Energy Projection	●○○○○○○
Fighting Skill	●●●○○○○

HAMMERHEAD

WEB FILE

Hammerhead can smash through nearly anything if he charges at it headfirst. He has a keen criminal mind and is skilled with guns, especially machine guns.

— POWER RATING —

Intelligence

Strength

Speed

Durability

Energy Projection

Fighting Skill

This flat-topped gangster earned his nickname after a brawl, when disgraced surgeon Jonas Harrow replaced his damaged skull with one made of steel. Hammerhead based his style on old gangster movies, and set out to clear the New York underworld of rivals, but usually found Spider-Man standing in his way.

Metal skull is his most powerful weapon.

Even Tougher

Hammerhead later received physical upgrades from Spider-Man's enemy Mr. Negative, in return for swearing total loyalty to him. He now has a skull and endo-skeleton made of adamantium, a nearly indestructible metal.

Hammerhead is a skilled brawler, but prefers to use his head to tackle problems.

"I don't play tough, bright eyes. I am tough!"

Hammerhead prefers fashions inspired by the 1920s.

Hammerhead has gotten meaner and nastier over the years, and he takes it out on Spider-Man.

HARRY OSBORN

The son of billionaire industrialist Norman Osborn, Harry Osborn became friends with Peter Parker when they were at Empire State University. Harry had a rocky relationship with his father, but when it seemed Norman had died battling Spider-Man, Harry became the second Green Goblin to avenge him.

"You're a good friend, Pete, but my family is none of your business."

Escaping His Father's Shadow
Harry was thought dead for a time, but reappeared to open a coffee shop in New York City and court socialite Lily Hollister. He later had a son with Peter Parker's friend Liz Allan, whom he named Normie. Harry is now a sworn enemy of his father's.

Harry has struggled for years over whether to embrace or reject his father's Green Goblin legacy.

Harry briefly became the armoured hero American Son, as part of a sinister plot orchestrated by his father Norman.

WEB FILE
Without the Green Goblin serum Harry has no superpowers, but he is highly intelligent and a skilled business leader.

— POWER RATING —

Intelligence	●●●●●●○
Strength	●●●○○○○
Speed	●●○○○○○
Durability	●●●○○○○
Energy Projection	●●○○○○○
Fighting Skill	●●●●○○○

HITMAN

WEB FILE

Hitman is a superb marksman, hunter, and hand-to-hand fighter. His jet aircraft HQ contains high-tech equipment.

—— POWER RATING ——

Intelligence	●●●●●●●●●
Strength	●●●●●●●●●●
Speed	●●○○○○○○○○
Durability	●●●○○○○○○○
Energy Projection	●●●●○○○○○○
Fighting Skill	●●●●●○○○○○

Burt Kenyon once saved the life of Frank Castle (the Punisher) when they were in the U.S. Marines, and pursued a similarly violent path by becoming a paid assassin for the Maggia crime families. As Hitman he tried to take down Spider-Man, leading to a showdown atop the Statue of Liberty.

Military training gave Hitman an advantage in combat.

Perilous Plunge

The Punisher, while tempted to repay his debt to his wounded former comrade-in-arms, chose to save Spider-Man instead. The Hitman fell from the Statue of Liberty into the dark waters below, apparently bringing about a permanent end to his career as an assassin.

Hitman carried spare ammo in bandoliers.

Criminals lived in fear of heroes like Spider-Man, but knew they could hire the Hitman to keep their operations safe.

"Nothing personal on my part, you understand. Just business!"

HOBGOBLIN

Billionaire fashion designer Roderick Kingsley felt vulnerable after being attacked by a rival. Craving strength, he took Norman Osborn's Green Goblin formula, and became the evil Hobgoblin. Others have since followed in Roderick's footsteps, making the Hobgoblin a foe who has plagued Spider-Man at every turn.

Every time Spider-Man thinks he has the Hobgoblin down for the count, the villain arises in a new form.

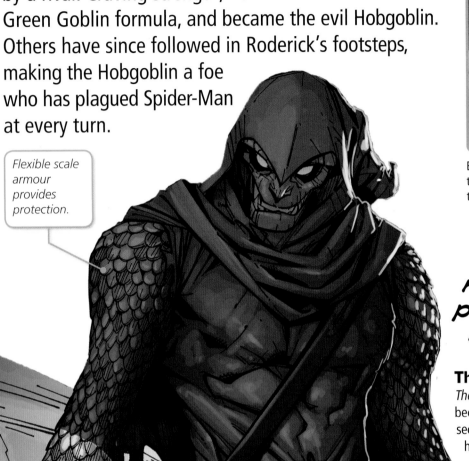

Flexible scale armour provides protection.

Pouches contain gas bombs and other explosives.

"The Green Goblin is no more, but in his place now stands the Hobgoblin!"

The Latest Villain
The Daily Bugle journalist Phil Urich became the latest Hobgoblin. When his secret identity was made public, he allied himself with the Green Goblin, pledging his services to further Osborn's crusade against Spider-Man.

WEB FILE
Green Goblin formula gives Hobgoblin superhuman abilities. He uses versions of Green Goblin's weapons and equipment, including Jack O'Lantern bombs, and a glider.

— POWER RATING —
Intelligence ●●●●●●○
Strength ●●●●●○○
Speed ●●●○○○○
Durability ●●●●○○○
Energy Projection ●●●○○○○
Fighting Skill ●●●●●○○

HOOD

WEB FILE

The Hood gets his powers from his magical cloak and boots. His cloak can render him invisible when he holds his breath, and his boots enable him to walk on air.

— POWER RATING —

Intelligence ●●●●●●●○○
Strength ●●●○○○○○○
Speed ●●○○○○○○○
Durability ●●●○○○○○○
Energy Projection ●●●●○○○○○
Fighting Skill ●●●●○○○○○

Petty crook Parker Robbins stole a mystical cloak and boots imbued with dark magic, which gave him the powers of invisibility and flight. Robbins used his powers to launch a new criminal career as the Hood, gathering a team of Super Villains to form a new criminal faction, and becoming an unwelcome thorn in Spider-Man's side.

Power Grab

The Hood made a move to take over the criminal territory controlled by rival crime boss Mister Negative. When Mister Negative resisted, a full-scale gang war erupted that Spider-Man was powerless to stop.

"I pride myself on being a forward thinker."

The Hood's cloak is a magical artifact stolen from a demon.

The Hood even brought dead villains back to life to serve as his foot soldiers.

He started out as a small-timer, but the Hood has gradually grown convinced of his ability to defeat even the strongest heroes.

HORIZON LABS

Horizon Labs was founded by Max Modell as a place where the world's best scientists could bring next-generation ideas to life. The team has also dealt with public emergencies, such as a city-wide outbreak of spider-virus. Peter Parker has been a Horizon Labs employee, inventing technology that benefits both Spider-Man and humankind.

Impressed by Peter's scientific knowledge during a tour of the facility, Horizon Labs' chief, Max Modell, offered him a job on the spot.

MEMBERS

1. **Grady Scraps:** Time-travel researcher.

2. **Sajani Jaffrey:** Expert in alien technology and biology.

3. **Bella Fishbach:** Expert in eco-technology.

4. **Max Modell:** Brilliant inventor and founder of Horizon Labs.

5. **Uatu Jackson:** Child genius with a gift for electronics.

"Attention all Horizon Staff. I have a project that requires a lot of brainpower."

Cutting Corners

Horizon Labs is considered a menace by J. Jonah Jameson, the new mayor of New York City. Although he knows its personnel are brilliant, their unauthorized experiments – such as a doorway that doubles as a portal through time – frequently violate the city's safety regulations.

Max Modell is the team's practical and spiritual leader.

HORNET

WEB FILE

A special serum gave Hornet great strength and insect-like wings. He could also project powerful bio-electric bursts that could stun or even kill.

— POWER RATING —

Intelligence	●●●●○○○○○○
Strength	●●●●○○○○○○
Speed	●●●●○○○○○○
Durability	●●●○○○○○○○
Energy Projection	●●●○○○○○○○
Fighting Skill	●●●○○○○○○○

Wheelchair-bound criminologist Scotty McDowell regained his mobility after a scientist spliced his DNA with an insect's as part of a revenge plot against Spider-Woman (Jessica Drew). As the costumed hero Hornet, he fought crooks using the power of flight and his electrical "hornet sting".

Wings used for hovering and bursts of speed.

Hornet-sting blasts can knock out opponents in an instant.

Heroic Inspiration

The operation that gave Scotty heroic powers was also designed to slowly turn him against his ally, Spider-Woman. When she realized that the scientist was using her friend to try to hurt her, Spider-Woman returned Scotty to his original state. Spider-Man later used the Hornet's name and costume to create an undercover identity.

"No living mortal can withstand the sting of the Hornet!"

In his role as a criminologist, Scotty McDowell did a lot to aid Jessica Drew in her Super Hero career as Spider-Woman.

HULK

With his battle cry "Hulk smash!", the Hulk is one of the strongest beings in existence. Gamma rays from an atom bomb test turned scientist Bruce Banner into the rampaging Hulk. He has switched between his two forms ever since – usually without his control. Spider-Man would rather help the Hulk, but sometimes he has to fight him!

When the Hulk serves with the Avengers, the team has a heavy hitter who can't be beaten.

Irradiated superhuman muscles.

"You talk too much, bug man!"

At War With Himself
Bruce Banner tries to remain in control of his transformations, but outbursts of pain and rage often trigger the emergence of the Hulk. At times, Bruce has been able to keep his highly intelligent mind active within the Hulk's unstoppable body.

A stomp of Hulk's foot can cause a minor earthquake.

WEB FILE
The Hulk has almost limitless strength. He can leap several miles in a single bound and his body heals almost instantly.

— POWER RATING —
Intelligence	●●●●●○○○○○
Strength	●●●●●●●●●●
Speed	●●○○○○○○○○
Durability	●●●●●●●○○○
Energy Projection	●●○○○○○○○○
Fighting Skill	●●●●○○○○○○

HUMAN FLY

SPIDEY STATUS
ENEMY

A crook who volunteered for an experiment to recover from a gunshot wound emerged as the Human Fly! The true extent of his powers emerged over time, and gradually transformed the Human Fly into a horrific monster. The Human Fly is easily one of Spider-Man's most disgusting foes.

WEB FILE

The Human Fly has the powers of a human-sized housefly, with the ability to stick to walls, remain airborne with buzzing, razor-sharp wings and spew acid from his mouth.

— POWER RATING —

Intelligence	●●●○○○○
Strength	●●●●○○○
Speed	●●●○○○○
Durability	●●●○○○○
Energy Projection	●●○○○○○
Fighting Skill	●●●○○○○

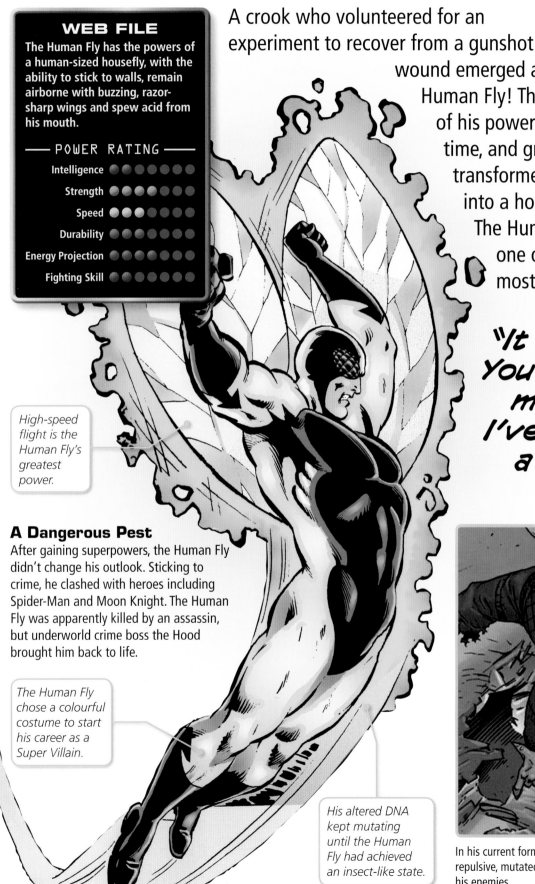

High-speed flight is the Human Fly's greatest power.

"It worked! You changed me, Doc! I've become a human fly!"

A Dangerous Pest

After gaining superpowers, the Human Fly didn't change his outlook. Sticking to crime, he clashed with heroes including Spider-Man and Moon Knight. The Human Fly was apparently killed by an assassin, but underworld crime boss the Hood brought him back to life.

The Human Fly chose a colourful costume to start his career as a Super Villain.

His altered DNA kept mutating until the Human Fly had achieved an insect-like state.

In his current form, the Human Fly is a repulsive, mutated horror who tries to eat his enemies.

HUMAN TORCH

Johnny Storm gained fire-controlling powers during the same cosmic accident that created the Fantastic Four. The most hot-headed member of the team, he likes to have fun and doesn't always take his responsibilities seriously. The Human Torch met Spider-Man when they were both teenagers, and despite some bickering they became good friends.

The Human Torch is flanked by his sister, Sue Storm Richards, and the Fantastic Four's leader Reed Richards.

"That's it, you animated insect! Fun's over!"

Fiery Friend
When they want to talk, Spider-Man and the Human Torch have a special meeting spot on top of the Statue of Liberty. During a time when the Human Torch was thought to be dead, Spider-Man took his place on the Fantastic Four.

Johnny Storm cries "Flame on!" when turning into the Human Torch.

When the Human Torch flies, he leaves flaming trails across the New York skyline.

WEB FILE
The Human Torch can control heat energy, cover his body with fiery plasma, fly and fire a powerful "nova burst."

— POWER RATING —
Intelligence	●●●●●○○
Strength	●●●●○○○
Speed	●●●●●●○
Durability	●●●○○○○
Energy Projection	●●●●●●○
Fighting Skill	●●●●●○○

HYDRO-MAN

WEB FILE

Hydro-Man can transform all or part of his body into a watery substance and emit powerful water blasts. He can also manipulate water outside his own body.

— POWER RATING —

Intelligence ●●●○○○○
Strength ●●●●○○○
Speed ●●●○○○○
Durability ●●●●●○○
Energy Projection ●●●●○○○
Fighting Skill ●●●○○○○

Accidentally knocked overboard into an experimental generator, cargo ship crewman Morris Bench morphed into a being made entirely of water. As Hydro-Man, he signed on with the Frightful Four and the Sinister Syndicate to fight Spider-Man, and even merged with Sandman to create a rampaging Mud-Thing.

Control over his molecules lets Hydro-Man take human form.

Running Water

Hydro-Man is difficult to damage, nearly impossible to contain, and can reconstitute himself from a single molecule. He has used his powers to travel through the New York City sewer system, searching for Spider-Man in order to set up an ambush.

Hydro-Man can convert any part of his body back to its liquid state at will.

Hydro-Man attempted to submerge Spider-Man within the waters of his body, hoping to doom the web-slinger to a watery grave.

HYPNO-HUSTLER

SPIDEY STATUS ENEMY

Lead singer of the Mercy Killers, the Hypno-Hustler uses special goggles and the mesmerizing sounds of his guitar and backup singers to turn his audience into obedient puppets. Spider-Man defeated him by removing the headphones that kept the Hypno-Hustler immune from his own effects.

Hypno-Hustler's big heist would have succeeded if Peter Parker hadn't been in the audience.

Convinces enemies they're fighting an unbeatable foe.

Mesmerizing Man

The Hypno-Hustler landed behind bars, but he escaped and improved his ability to generate hypnotic soundwaves, even hiring the Tinkerer to design new pieces of sonic equipment. Most recently, the Hypno-Hustler had a run-in with Spider-Man and Deadpool that ended with his defeat.

WEB FILE

Hypno-Hustler's guitar can produce hypnotic soundwaves. He and his band the Mercy Killers can hypnotize audiences to do their will.

—— POWER RATING ——

Intelligence	●●●●●○○○○○
Strength	●●●○○○○○○○
Speed	●●○○○○○○○○
Durability	●●●○○○○○○○
Energy Projection	●●●●○○○○○○
Fighting Skill	●●●●●○○○○○

ICEMAN

Bobby Drake developed ice powers thanks to his mutant genetics, but he learned to control those powers as a founding member of the X-Men. For a time, Spider-Man teamed up with Iceman and another young hero, Firestar, as a crime-fighting trio.

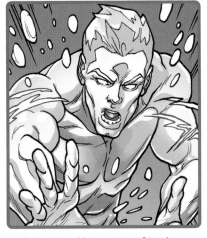

Spider-Man and his amazing friends Iceman and Firestar battled villains as a super-team.

Spidey and Iceman are about the same age.

"Web-Head, do your thing, but leave some for me!"

Chilly Rivalry

During one of their early encounters, Spider-Man and Iceman fought each other when Iceman believed that the wall-crawler had kidnapped an innocent woman. After working out their differences, the two heroes saved Robbie Robertson from a gang of thugs.

WEB FILE

Iceman can freeze anything he touches and manipulate the water vapor in the air to form weapons from ice. He can race along on ice slides he creates for himself.

—— POWER RATING ——

Intelligence ●●●●○○○○○○
Strength ●●●●○○○○○○
Speed ●●●●○○○○○○
Durability ●●●○○○○○○○
Energy Projection ●●●●○○○○○○
Fighting Skill ●●●●○○○○○○

73

IRON MAN

Billionaire Tony Stark, alias Iron Man, is an engineering genius. After building his first suit of armour to escape from foreign captivity, Tony has designed many more Iron Man battlesuits for different missions. Iron Man is a founding member of the Avengers and a mentor to Spider-Man.

Tony Stark is one of the world's greatest inventors, and one of the few heroes whose civilian identity is more famous than his costumed alter-ego.

Making More Armour

As a gift, Tony Stark provided Spider-Man with a new "spider armour" costume based on his previous Iron Man designs. Later, copies of the armoured costume were provided to the members of the government-sponsored team known as the Scarlet Spiders.

A miniaturized reactor provides the suit's power source.

Spider-Man never knows what new gadgets Iron Man is going to try next.

"Come on Peter, stay with me!"

WEB FILE

Tony Stark's Iron Man armour gives him superhuman strength and durability. Jet-powered boots enable him to fly. His gauntlets fire repulsor beams and a chest uni-beam fires energy blasts.

POWER RATING

Intelligence	●●●●●●○
Strength	●●●●●○○
Speed	●●●○○○○
Durability	●●●●●○○
Energy Projection	●●●●○○○
Fighting Skill	●●●●●○○

J. JONAH JAMESON

When Jameson was elected as mayor, Spider-Man knew he would soon face more harassment than ever before.

Even Spider-Man's worst foes don't seem as dedicated to his downfall as J. Jonah Jameson. The former Editor-in-Chief of *The Daily Bugle* believes the wall-crawler is a public menace. For years, Jonah led a smear campaign against Spider-Man, unaware that Peter Parker worked for *The Bugle* as a photographer.

"I want results, not excuses!"

Mister Mayor
Believing himself to be the best man for the job, J. Jonah Jameson left *The Daily Bugle* to run for mayor of New York City. He won, and one of his first acts was the creation of an "Anti-Spider Patrol" police taskforce.

J. Jonah Jameson thinks Spider-Man is a dangerous publicity-seeker.

J. J. Jameson leads by example, and was the hardest-working person at The Daily Bugle.

WEB FILE

His forceful personality makes Jameson a formidable boss and a tenacious opponent. He is a master of media manipulation.

— POWER RATING —

Intelligence	●●●●○○○
Strength	●●●○○○○
Speed	●●○○○○○
Durability	●●●○○○○
Energy Projection	●○○○○○○
Fighting Skill	●●●●○○○

JACK O'LANTERN

Ex-C.I.A. agent Jason Macendale became costumed mercenary Jack O'Lantern, with a flaming pumpkin head as his grotesque trademark. Later, Jason temporarily became the Hobgoblin, allowing the Jack O'Lantern identity to pass to new bearers.

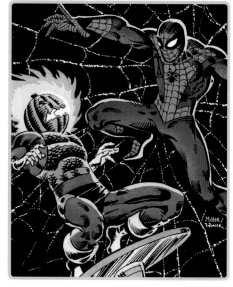

Spidey uses his webs to slow down the high-flying villain, but Jack O'Lantern is too well-trained to be led into an ambush.

Gauntlets fire energy blasts.

Killer Criminal

The current Jack O'Lantern is a nameless master assassin who uses weapons and vehicles that are similar to those of the Green Goblin. His advanced training and lack of mercy makes him even more lethal than previous incarnations of the villain.

Grenades can spray smoke or toxic gasses.

Jack O'Lantern rides a flying broom.

WEB FILE

Jack O'Lantern carries gas-filled grenades and electric wrist-blasters. He is an expert with a variety of weapons and combat techniques.

— POWER RATING —

Intelligence	●●●●●○○○○○
Strength	●●●○○○○○○○
Speed	●●○○○○○○○○
Durability	●●●○○○○○○○
Energy Projection	●●●●○○○○○○
Fighting Skill	●●●●●○○○○○

JACKAL

Biology professor Miles Warren perfected the forbidden science of human cloning. As he lost his sanity, Miles transformed himself into the Jackal. He created the horrific Carrion, the later-repentant clone Kaine, and the Peter-Parker duplicate Ben Reilly (the Scarlet Spider).

WEB FILE
Jackal's scientific genius and knowledge of cloning has brought him superhuman strength. His claws are razor-sharp and tipped with poison; gas bombs are his favourite weapons.

POWER RATING
Intelligence	●●●●●●
Strength	●●●○○○
Speed	●●○○○○
Durability	●●○○○○
Energy Projection	●●○○○○
Fighting Skill	●●●●○○

"You are my science experiment."

Mad Science
The Jackal is a brilliant but demented geneticist. In addition to his mad cloning experiments, he caused an outbreak of spider-powers across New York by creating a virus carried by bedbugs. It infected every resident of Manhattan Island, unleashing mayhem on a vast scale.

Originally fully human, the Jackal has gradually transformed into his current state.

The Jackal has known Peter Parker since his college days, and has knowledge of Spidey that other Super Villains would kill to possess.

SPIDEY STATUS

JACKPOT

When Spider-Man saw Jackpot's red hair, he grew suspicious that she might be Mary Jane Watson! He was relieved to find that the hair was actually a wig and Jackpot was a woman named Sara Ehret. Sara wanted to give up being a Super Hero, but Spidey convinced her to use her powers to help others.

WEB FILE

Jackpot's mutant growth hormone gives her superhuman strength, speed and endurance. Her body is so tough that she is effectively bulletproof.

— POWER RATING —

Intelligence	●●●●●○○○○○
Strength	●●●●○○○○○○
Speed	●●●○○○○○○○
Durability	●●●●○○○○○○
Energy Projection	●●○○○○○○○○
Fighting Skill	●●●○○○○○○○

"Just call me Miss Lucky."

Jackpot's costume has been passed from one wearer to another.

Team-ups between Spider-Man and Jackpot haven't always ended well, since Jackpot is still learning the ropes and doesn't always make the right choices in the heat of battle.

Back in Action

When Sara Ehret left the role of Jackpot, she sold the name and costume to a second woman, Alana Jobson. But Spider-Man's heroic example inspired Sara to return as Jackpot and she battled the villains Boomerang and the Rose.

Boots are reinforced for extra grip on slippery surfaces.

JEAN DEWOLFF

NYPD captain Jean DeWolff loved the cars and clothes of the 1930s. She broke ranks with her colleagues by declaring her support for Spider-Man. Sadly, she died when targeted by the Sin-Eater, leaving the wall-crawler with a heavy heart and one less friend in high places.

Capt. DeWolff's no-nonsense attitude put her on the fast track to promotion.

"Read him his rights, boys!"

Jean DeWolff always listened to Spider-Man, even when her colleagues wouldn't. After receiving a tip-off from the wall-crawler, Capt. DeWolff would lead a squad to investigate.

Jean DeWolff had an eccentric love for classic fashions.

A Life of Service
Jean DeWolff's demanding father pushed her to join the police force. She was on track to become police commissioner, until the Sin-Eater cut her down in the prime of her career. Spider-Man and Daredevil teamed up to solve her murder.

WEB FILE
Capt. DeWolff had police officer training, including crime scene investigation, unarmed combat, and the use of firearms.

— POWER RATING —
Intelligence ●●●○○○○
Strength ●●●○○○○
Speed ●●○○○○○
Durability ●●○○○○○
Energy Projection ●○○○○○○
Fighting Skill ●●●●○○○

JOHN JAMESON

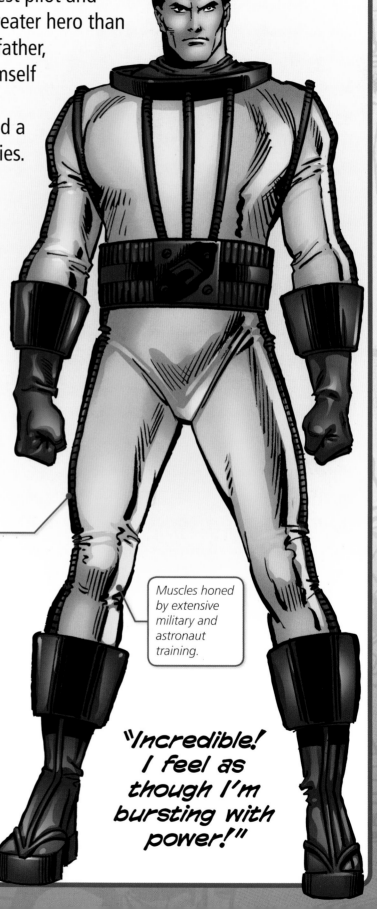

**SPIDEY STATUS
NEUTRAL**

Colonel John Jameson, test pilot and NASA astronaut, was a greater hero than Spider-Man – at least according to his father, *The Daily Bugle's* J. J. Jameson. John himself never made such claims, having a deep respect for the web-slinger. He remained a voice of reason between the two enemies.

Altered Astronaut

Exposure to outer space artifacts led Jameson to experience a series of strange mutations. At first he exhibited incredible strength – so much so that he was forced to wear a space suit to contain it. Later, in his most famous transformation, Jameson changed into the werewolf-like Man-Wolf.

WEB FILE

John Jameson is an astronaut and test pilot, trained in unarmed combat and with weapons.

— POWER RATING —

Intelligence	●●●●●○○
Strength	●●●●○○○
Speed	●●○○○○○
Durability	●●●○○○○
Energy Projection	●○○○○○○
Fighting Skill	●●●●○○○

Containment suit built to keep his strength in check.

Muscles honed by extensive military and astronaut training.

At first, John fought Spider-Man because his father had said that he was a dangerous outlaw. But John was soon to learn that he and Spidey shared similar values.

"Incredible! I feel as though I'm bursting with power!"

JONAS HARROW

"When you wake you'll be a new man—gifted beyond your wildest dreams!"

Chased out of the medical profession for his horrific experiments, Jonas Harrow put his skills to use in the criminal underworld. His test cases have included the physical augmentations of Spider-Man foes Hammerhead and Kangaroo, and the attempted mind control of Will O'The Wisp.

Delusions of Grandeur

Jonas Harrow dabbled in mind-control until Spider-Man stopped his plans. He later invented a device that could drain the powers of Super Heroes, and tried to use it to gain power in the criminal underworld. Harrow's efforts led to his apparent death in a revenge attack by former employer the Hood, whom he had betrayed.

Jonas Harrow's greatest assets are his skilled surgeon's hands.

Goggles have built-in magnifiers for use in complex procedures.

Sterile surgical scrubs.

Harrow is an expert in human biology and neuroscience. His mind-controlling technology involves placing implants in the brains of his victims.

WEB FILE

Jonas Harrow is a scientific genius specializing in cybernetics, mechanics and surgery.

— POWER RATING —

Intelligence	●●●●●○
Strength	●●●○○○○
Speed	●○○○○○○
Durability	●●○○○○○
Energy Projection	●○○○○○○
Fighting Skill	●●○○○○○

JUDAS TRAVELLER

Judas Traveller was a criminal psychologist until a nervous breakdown triggered his mental powers. Norman Osborn used him as a pawn in a plot to take down Spider-Man, manipulating Judas's ability to cloud people's minds to put Spider-Man and his clone, Ben Reilly, through a series of ordeals.

Mental powers include mesmerism and mind-reading.

Though he seemed to possess abilities that rivalled those of Doctor Strange, Judas Traveller has since withdrawn from the public eye.

Judas the Judge
In his biggest scheme, Judas Traveller took over the Ravencroft Institute for the Criminally Insane. With the inmates as his jury and Carnage as his prosecutor, Judas Traveller put Spider-Man on trial to determine whether the wall-crawler was worthy of calling himself a hero.

WEB FILE
Former psychologist Judas Traveller can read minds and alter people's perception of reality.

— POWER RATING —

Intelligence	●●●●●●○○
Strength	●●●○○○○○
Speed	●●○○○○○○
Durability	●●●●○○○○
Energy Projection	●●●●●○○○
Fighting Skill	●●●●○○○○

JUGGERNAUT

WEB FILE

Juggernaut has superhuman strength and stamina, and is virtually invulnerable and unstoppable. His helmet protects him against psionic attack and his armor has mystical power.

— POWER RATING —

Intelligence	●●●●●●○○○○
Strength	●●●●●●●●●●
Speed	●●●○○○○○○○
Durability	●●●●●●●●●●
Energy Projection	●○○○○○○○○○
Fighting Skill	●●●●●●○○○○

While serving with the U.S. Army in Korea, Cain Marko unwittingly found and entered a lost temple. Unable to control himself, he grabbed a mystic ruby, and was transformed into the Juggernaut – a villain who cannot be stopped once he gets going.

Stopping the Unstoppable

When the Juggernaut kidnapped Madame Web, Spider-Man did everything in his power to stop the villain. Realizing that he would have to use brains instead of brawn against such a powerful foe, he won by trapping the Juggernaut in a pool of wet cement.

Virtually indestructible Magical armour.

Juggernaut does not feel pain or tiredness.

"You got lucky the first time. Now it's my turn!"

Even if he has been restrained for experimentation, the mighty Juggernaut is only ever a temporary captive.

KAINE

Attempting a perfect clone of Peter Parker, the Jackal created the obsessed vigilante, Kaine. This clone had a scarred face and the ability to give foes the "Mark of Kaine" with his burning touch. Though Kaine died in a plot by the heirs of Kraven the Hunter, he returned as one of the undead.

A Destiny of His Own
Kaine has made many attempts to emerge from the shadow of Peter Parker. After helping to end the spider-virus outbreak in New York City, Kaine – now cured of his facial scarring – relocated to Houston, Texas. There he found his own identity as a Super Hero.

Enhanced wall-crawling powers.

"I know you, Spider-Man, better than you know yourself."

Costume hides his identity.

WEB FILE
Kaine has Spider-Man's superhuman abilities and channels burning energy through his hands. His "spider-sense" is imperfect, but allows him to glimpse the future.

— POWER RATING —

Intelligence	●●●●●○○
Strength	●●●●●●○
Speed	●●●○○○○
Durability	●●●●○○○
Energy Projection	●●○○○○○
Fighting Skill	●●●●●●○

Kaine and Spider-Man haven't always gotten along. Far more troubled than Peter's other clone, Ben Reilly, Kaine has led a difficult life.

KANGAROO

WEB FILE

Kangaroo's armoured suit gives him superhuman strength and amazing leaping abilities. The suit also includes a prehensile tail and pouch cannon.

— POWER RATING —

Intelligence ●●●●●○○○○○
Strength ●●●●●●○○○○
Speed ●●●○○○○○○○
Durability ●●●●○○○○○○
Energy Projection ●●○○○○○○○○
Fighting Skill ●●●●●○○○○○

Brian Hibbs became the criminal known as Kangaroo, outfitting himself with an armoured suit featuring a pouch-mounted cannon and a tail that could knock down walls. This Kangaroo found like-minded allies in the villains Spot, Grizzly, and the Gibbon.

"With my new kangaroo battle-armour, I'll be able to stop any Super Hero in town!"

Armour designed by villain named the Tinkerer.

Suit's strength powered by hydraulics.

Chasing Dreams

The Kangaroo drew his inspiration from a previous villain, an Australian-born brawler (and possible latent mutant) also known as the Kangaroo. As the second Kangaroo, Hibbs uses mechanized weaponry to make up for his lack of super powers.

Kangaroo tail is dangerous to those who get too close.

KINGPIN

The boss of New York's crime scene, the Kingpin worked his way up the underworld ladder, bumping off rivals and making enemies of the Maggia crime syndicate. The Kingpin is one of Spider-Man's most powerful enemies, and he has ruthlessly targeted those closest to Peter.

His bulk, often mistaken for fat, is pure muscle.

Untouchable

The Kingpin is prepared for anything, and can outwit almost any opponent. Spider-Man has been forced to back down from busting him in the past, after realizing that he didn't have enough evidence to send the crime boss to jail permanently.

The Kingpin dresses in the finest suits money can buy.

Even with Spidey's super-strength, it can be tough for him to get the upper hand on the Kingpin.

"I want every mob in the city to know— the Kingpin is ready to take over!"

WEB FILE

Kingpin has a brilliant criminal mind and formidable hand-to-hand combat skills. His huge body is almost solid muscle.

— POWER RATING —

Intelligence	●●●●●○
Strength	●●●●●●
Speed	●●○○○○
Durability	●●●●○○
Energy Projection	●○○○○○
Fighting Skill	●●●●○○

KRAVEN THE HUNTER

WEB FILE

Kraven is an expert tracker and hunter. His strength and stamina is enhanced by mystical jungle potions, which also extend his life.

— POWER RATING —

Intelligence	●●●●●●○
Strength	●●●●●●○○
Speed	●●●●○○○○
Durability	●●●●●○○○
Energy Projection	●○○○○○○
Fighting Skill	●●●●●●○

Sergei Kravinoff was determined to become the greatest hunter who had ever lived. However, he knew he could never truly be the best if he couldn't defeat Spider-Man. Calling himself Kraven the Hunter, he relentlessly pursued the wall-crawler.

"I came here to hunt the most dangerous game of all!"

Kraven's furred vest resembles the mane of a lion.

Kraven's strength has been boosted beyond human limits.

A spiked belt helps when grappling foes.

Kraven often commands animals to do his bidding, including leopards, tigers, and other predatory cats.

An Ending and a Beginning

In what he considered his "Last Hunt", Kraven finally beat Spider-Man and then took his own life. His wife Sasha Kravinoff gathered the family to hunt Spider-Man's allies and perform a mystic ritual to enable Kraven to return from the dead.

LEAP-FROG

Failed inventor Vinnie Patilio turned to crime after discovering he could use electrical coils to jump over rooftops. Fashioning an amphibian-themed costume, he became Leap-Frog and battled Daredevil and Spider-Man. Leap-Frog isn't much of a threat, but he hopes to make it to the criminal big leagues someday.

To his credit, Leap-Frog never considered himself a threat on the level of Doctor Octopus. If Spider-Man shows up, he'd rather run than fight.

Electrical coils permit power-jumps.

Ageing body is in poor condition.

"Just once I'd like to use these leaping coils without taking my life into my hands!"

It Runs in the Family

Leap-Frog has a son, Frog-Man, who is one of Spider-Man's biggest fans. At the invitation of Frog-Man, Spider-Man spent an evening at the Patilio home. After dinner, both Leap-Frog and Frog-Man leaped into action to help the wall-crawler defeat the White Rabbit.

WEB FILE

Leap-Frog can make massive leaps owing to electrical coils in his boots. His suit's exoskeleton enhances his strength.

— POWER RATING —

Intelligence	●●●●●●○
Strength	●●●○○○○
Speed	●○○○○○○
Durability	●●●●○○○
Energy Projection	●●●○○○○
Fighting Skill	●●●●○○○

LIGHTMASTER

WEB FILE

Lightmaster can absorb or generate light, create solid objects from light and fly. He is also immune to telepathy.

POWER RATING

Intelligence	●●●●●●○
Strength	●●○○○○○
Speed	●●●●○○○
Durability	●●●○○○○
Energy Projection	●●●●●○○
Fighting Skill	●●○○○○○

Dismayed by budget cuts, physics professor Dr. Edward Lansky became Lightmaster. A special suit allowed him to absorb and emit photons, and he worked with Kraven the Hunter and Tarantula while extorting city officials into providing funding for university programmes. Spider-Man ended Lightmaster's criminal campaign.

"Lightmaster's vengeance shall be swift and merciless!"

Lights Out

An accident later transformed Lightmaster into a being composed entirely of energy. He has tried a number of schemes in order to regain his physical form, including an attempt to steal the light-controlling powers of mutant hero Dazzler. Spider-Man and Dazzler teamed up to beat Lightmaster.

Now that Lightmaster has become a being of living light, he is more dangerous than ever. However, his energies fade if he pushes himself too much.

Containment suit enables absorption of electromagnetic energy.

Uses his powers to fly.

LIVING BRAIN

The artificial intelligence of the Living Brain could deduce the answer to any question, including "Who is Spider-Man?" Luckily for Peter Parker, when the robot came to Midtown High School, it went on a rampage before it could reveal its findings.

"Why was unit programmed with pain receptors? Whyyyyy?"

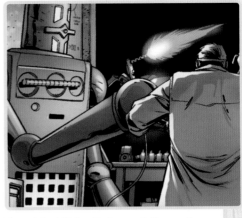

The original Living Brain, revolutionary for its time, has been upgraded over the years to keep pace with advances in processing power and artificial intelligence.

Valuable Hardware

Since its first appearance at Midtown High School, the Living Brain has been upgraded with a speech synthesizer and an improved processor. Recently the Living Brain served as a member of the Sinister Six, using its advanced intelligence to calculate success probabilities and escape vectors.

Damage to its controls made the Living Brain malfunction.

WEB FILE

The Living Brain robot can outthink any human being and is incapable of forgetting anything. It fights by rapidly spinning its arms and body.

— POWER RATING —

Intelligence ●●●●●●●
Strength ●●●●●●
Speed ●●●●
Durability ●●●●
Energy Projection ●●
Fighting Skill ●●●

LIZ ALLAN

WEB FILE

Liz is a skilled corporate leader with experience in international business. Close encounters with Super Villains have left her with above-average fighting skills.

── POWER RATING ──

Intelligence	●●●●●●○
Strength	●●○○○○○
Speed	●○○○○○○
Durability	●●○○○○○
Energy Projection	●○○○○○○
Fighting Skill	●●●○○○○

Liz Allan was one of the most popular students at Midtown High School, unlike shy Peter Parker. But Liz saw Peter's kind heart and became his close friend. She spent years caring for her stepbrother Mark Raxton, the Molten Man, and remains a key ally of Spider-Man.

"I know Spidey. He's a friend."

Liz Allan has achieved great success in the science and research industry.

The most important person in Liz Allan's life is her son, Normie. She hopes that he will take control of the Allan business enterprise when he is old enough.

Family Business

Liz Allan married Harry Osborn, and had a son, Normie (named after Harry's father Norman Osborn). Accustomed to wealth and power, Liz ran the Osborn corporate empire for a time. She has since taken control of the family business, Allan Chemical, and merged it with Horizon Labs to create a powerful new company, Alchemax.

LIZARD

Dr. Curt Connors' secret formula based on reptile DNA restored his missing arm, but it also mutated him into his gruesome alter-ego, the Lizard! Spider-Man first faced the Lizard in the Florida Everglades, but the monster followed him to New York City for many more showdowns.

"The excitement... the fear... changing me into—the Lizard!"

When the Lizard's primal, reptilian brain is in control, Dr. Curt Connors can't recognize his friend Spider-Man or show him mercy.

Suppressing the Predator
Curt Connors is sometimes a friend to Spider-Man, but only when he is able to keep his animal side under control. The Lizard joined with Doctor Octopus to steal Lily Hollister's baby away from her, but when Curt Connors' good nature resurfaced, the Lizard handed the baby over to Spider-Man.

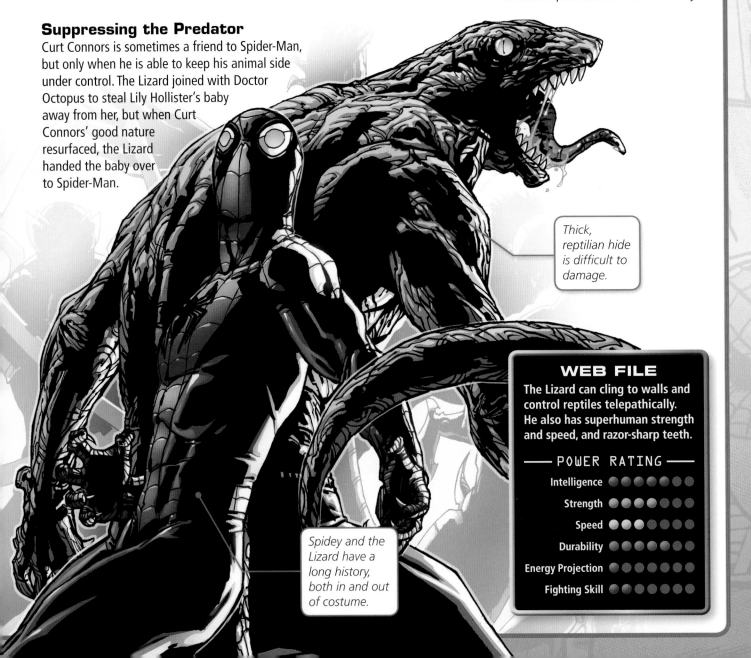

Thick, reptilian hide is difficult to damage.

Spidey and the Lizard have a long history, both in and out of costume.

WEB FILE
The Lizard can cling to walls and control reptiles telepathically. He also has superhuman strength and speed, and razor-sharp teeth.

— POWER RATING —
Intelligence	●●●●○○○
Strength	●●●●●○○
Speed	●●●○○○○
Durability	●●●●○○○
Energy Projection	●○○○○○○
Fighting Skill	●●●●○○○

LOBO BROTHERS

Carlos and Eduardo Lobo were mutants, able to transform into werewolves at will. When they formed a gang that threatened the Kingpin's criminal empire, Spider-Man tried to defuse the gang war that resulted, but was unsuccessful and the situation ended tragically.

When the Lobo Brothers attacked at the same time, Spider-Man wasn't able to guard against both threats.

Sharpened animal senses help the brothers hunt their foes.

End of a Partnership

The Daily Bugle's Glory Grant fell in love with Eduardo as the gang war escalated. Eduardo was ultimately killed, accidentally shot with a silver bullet fired by Glory herself. She claimed she had been aiming at Spider-Man, and she blamed the wall-crawler for Eduardo's death.

The brothers share a weakness to weapons made of silver.

WEB FILE

In werewolf form, Eduardo and Carlos possessed superhuman strength, speed, hearing, and smell, making them deadly foes.

— POWER RATING —

Intelligence	●●●○○○○
Strength	●●●●○○○
Speed	●●●●○○○
Durability	●●●○○○○
Energy Projection	●○○○○○○
Fighting Skill	●●●●○○○

LOOTER

Disgraced scientist Norton Fester finally got a lucky break when his examination of a meteorite released a cloud of strange gasses. Norton found that the gasses had honed his body to peak physical perfection, and he engaged in big-ticket robberies as the Looter. Luckily, Spider-Man is usually there to stop him.

More recently, the Looter has also gone by the alias of Meteor Man. He uses balloons to escape from the scenes of his crimes.

Special Treasures

The Looter needs special meteorites in order to maintain his physical abilities, and getting more of them has become his obsession. His focus on them has allowed Spider-Man to work out the pattern of the crimes and anticipate the Looter's next move.

"There it is—a safe full of bounty money just waiting to be looted!"

Meteorite of the kind that transformed the Looter.

The Looter cannot duplicate the meteorite's effects artificially.

WEB FILE

Looter has superhuman strength, and can survive falls from great heights. He uses a variety of gadgets of his own invention, including a blinding dazzle gun.

— POWER RATING —

Intelligence	●●●●●○○○
Strength	●●●●●○○○
Speed	●●○○○○○○
Durability	●●●●○○○○
Energy Projection	●●●○○○○○
Fighting Skill	●●●●○○○○

LUKE CAGE

Luke Cage is an excellent field leader, and puts his skills to good use with the New Avengers.

Framed for a crime he didn't commit, Luke Cage underwent a cruel experiment in prison that gave him superhuman strength and durability, including bulletproof skin. As Power Man he operated a "Heroes for Hire" business with martial artist Iron Fist, and he often helped Spider-Man stop street-level crimes.

Two-Fisted Fighter
Luke Cage later dropped the Power Man identity and signed on with Spider-Man as a founding member of the New Avengers. They have fought side by side against Super Villains and even an alien invasion.

"Name's Luke Cage. I'm with the Avengers."

Nearly indestructible, Luke Cage prefers up-close combat.

WEB FILE

Thanks to a serum similar to Captain America's, Luke Cage has superhuman strength, stamina and durability. A superb athlete, he taught himself unarmed combat techniques.

— POWER RATING —

Intelligence	●●●○○○○○
Strength	●●●●○○○○
Speed	●●○○○○○○
Durability	●●●●●●○○
Energy Projection	●○○○○○○○
Fighting Skill	●●●●○○○○

MADAME WEB

Blind and paralyzed Cassandra Webb possesses the mutant ability to read minds. As the fortune teller Madame Web she passed information to Spider-Man concerning his cases, and she also served as a mentor to Mattie Franklin, the fourth Spider-Woman.

Madame Web's ties with Spider-Man made her a target of the Kravinoff family, who tried to use her to control Spidey's future.

Madame Web could see into the past, present, and future.

Her spider-like chair was also a life-support system.

Transformations
In a mystic ceremony known as the Gathering of Five, Madame Web gained a more youthful appearance and enhanced mobility. She apparently died during Charlotte Witter's brief turn as a monstrous Spider-Woman hybrid, and passed her psychic gifts to Julia Carpenter.

WEB FILE
Madame Web had great telepathic powers and can predict future events. She can appear to others in spirit form. She depends on a cybernetic web to stay alive.

— POWER RATING —
Intelligence ●●●●●●○
Strength ●○○○○○○
Speed ●○○○○○○
Durability ●●○○○○○
Energy Projection ●●○○○○○
Fighting Skill ●●●●○○○

MAGGIA

The Maggia extort local businesses and violently protect their turf.

The Maggia is a criminal consortium of influential families. Led by the Silvermane, Hammerhead, and Nefaria families, the Maggia syndicate is an enemy of Spider-Man and the forces of law and order in New York City .

Agents Everywhere

Spider-Man has fought the Maggia's agents dozens of times, even though they often keep their true allegiance a secret. The Maggia gained its lofty criminal status by always keeping its schemes in shadow, leaving the police with no evidence to use for prosecution.

"The Maggia act first and ask questions later."

2

3

1

MEMBERS

1. **Silvermane:** Criminal mastermind; cybog body gives him superhuman strength, speed and durability.

2. **Count Nefaria:** Criminal scientist; body is scientifically enhanced to give him vast strength, but makes him a vampire.

3. **Hammerhead:** Super-strong crime boss with an adamantium cranium.

MAN-WOLF

On the moon, astronaut John Jameson picked up a gem whose energies morphed him into the Man-Wolf! At first John could not control his werewolf-like alter-ego, but he eventually managed to harness his powers for heroic causes, including preventing his father, J. J. Jameson, from capturing Spider-Man.

WEB FILE

Man-Wolf possesses superhuman strength, durability, agility, reflexes, and the heightened senses of a wolf.

— POWER RATING —

Intelligence	●●●●●●○○○○
Strength	●●●●●●●○○○
Speed	●●●○○○○○○○
Durability	●●●●●●○○○○
Energy Projection	●●○○○○○○○○
Fighting Skill	●●●●●●○○○○

Armour and weapons come from an alternate dimension.

Wild Side

John Jameson has struggled with his Man-Wolf identity. When the moon is full, Man-Wolf's savage side can sometimes overwhelm his ability to stay in control. When Spider-Man fought to contain a virus that accelerated the animalistic powers of people like the Lizard, Man-Wolf became one of the virus's victims.

John Jameson can't always control his Man-Wolf side, leading to conflicts with Spider-Man. Only by travelling to an alternate dimension is he able to retain his human intelligence while in his animal form.

MARCY KANE

At Empire State University, Peter Parker became friends with, and occasionally dated, biophysics teaching assistant Marcy Kane. Peter kept his super-hero identity secret from Marcy, unaware that she had one of her own – she came from beyond the stars!

An alien from the planet Contraxia, Marcy came to Earth to seek ways to save her world, whose sun was dying.

Knowledge of extraterrestrial science helped Marcy get her university post.

"Flattery will get you absolutely nowhere, Mr. Parker!"

Close Encounters

Marcy Kane, whose original name was Kania, arrived on Earth looking for a way to reignite the dying sun of her homeworld, Contraxia. Operating undercover at Empire State University, Marcy learned from brilliant scientists like Peter Parker while investigating experimental technologies.

Marcy's plain and simple wardrobe fit in with her role as a teacher.

None of her colleagues guessed that she was really an alien.

WEB FILE

Marcy is an alien from the planet Contraxia with an extensive knowledge of extraterrestrial science. She is a trained undercover agent.

— POWER RATING —

Intelligence	●●●●●●●
Strength	●●●○○○○
Speed	●●○○○○○
Durability	●●●○○○○
Energy Projection	●●●○○○○
Fighting Skill	●●●○○○○

MARY JANE WATSON

Peter Parker didn't know how he could ever settle down with a fun-loving, free spirit like Mary Jane Watson, but she proved to be the love of his life. MJ's feisty personality complements Peter's seriousness, and their love has persisted through the years.

MJ works as an actress and model.

In their first meeting, Mary Jane amazed Peter with her good looks. He soon grew to love her attitude, too.

Peter Meets His Match

Peter resisted the efforts of his Aunt May to hook him up with the girl next door, but changed his mind once he met Mary Jane. The two began dating following the tragic death of Peter's girlfriend Gwen Stacy. On the night that Peter's uncle was murdered, MJ saw Peter leaving his house dressed as Spider-Man and guessed his secret, although she hid her discovery from him for a long time. Peter trusts her completely, and has saved her life many times.

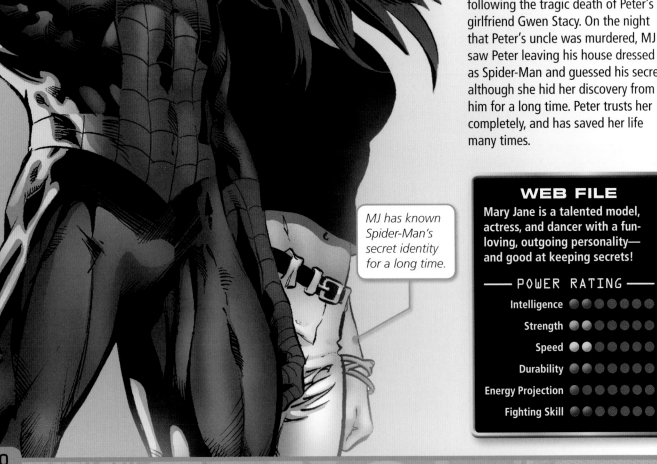

MJ has known Spider-Man's secret identity for a long time.

WEB FILE

Mary Jane is a talented model, actress, and dancer with a fun-loving, outgoing personality—and good at keeping secrets!

— POWER RATING —

Intelligence ●●●●●○○○
Strength ●●○○○○○○
Speed ●●●○○○○○
Durability ●○○○○○○○
Energy Projection ●○○○○○○○
Fighting Skill ●●●○○○○○

MARY AND RICHARD PARKER

Raised by his Aunt May and Uncle Ben, Peter Parker never knew his real parents, CIA agents Richard and Mary Parker. They died in a plane crash with many believing they had been traitors. Years later, Peter cleared their names.

"I never even knew them, but they gave their lives for America!"

Mary and Richard Parker loved their baby boy, but didn't live to see him grow up.

Heroes to the End

Posing as traitors to their country, the Parkers infiltrated a secret organization run by Captain America's arch-enemy the Red Skull. But tragically, the Red Skull discovered that his new operatives were actually double agents, and he arranged for the Parkers to die in an air crash.

Mary and Richard were trained by the U.S. government.

WEB FILE

Richard and Mary Parker were trained operatives working for U.S. security. They were both highly intelligent, and while no stronger than normal, physically fit adults, were exceptionally skilled at hand-to-hand combat and with firearms.

MASSACRE

When a guilt-ridden Spider-Man vowed that no one would die on his watch, emotionless killer Marcus Lyman arose as Massacre to challenge his claim. Massacre carved a path of destruction across the city. Spider-Man defeated him, but Massacre soon came back for more.

WEB FILE
Shrapnel embedded in his brain turned Lyman into a ruthless killer. He is an expert with firearms and explosive devices.

POWER RATING

Intelligence	●●●●○○○○○○
Strength	●●●○○○○○○○
Speed	●●○○○○○○○○
Durability	●●●○○○○○○○
Energy Projection	●●○○○○○○○○
Fighting Skill	●●●●●○○○○○

Head trauma left Massacre utterly without empathy.

Hostage Crisis
Massacre got the attention of the police by seizing prisoners and threatening their lives, even setting off a bomb inside a crowded bank. When Spider-Man first confronted Massacre, he suffered a gunshot wound. After armouring up, Spider-Man managed to defeat Massacre by using magnetic webbing.

"I'm not playing by your rules. You're playing by mine."

Massacre is determined to go out in a blaze of glory, and doesn't care how many innocent lives he threatens along the way.

MENACE

Lily Hollister had all the right connections, including a friendship with Carlie Cooper, a romance with Harry Osborn, and a father running for mayor of New York City. No one knew that Lily also adventured as the villainous Menace, using Green Goblin serum to transform her body and wielding an arsenal of Goblin-related weaponry.

Spider-Man fought Menace when she arrived on the scene, not realizing that Norman Osborn would soon recruit her as a powerful new member in his schemes.

"Menace is back, Manhattan!"

Green Goblin serum gives Lily a devilish appearance.

Joining the Family

Menace fought Spider-Man and earned the respect of Norman Osborn, who welcomed her as a new member of the Green Goblin family. She formed an alliance with Norman against her ex-lover, Harry. Menace later had Harry Osborn's baby, but left the child with Spider-Man, fearing that she was an unfit mother. She later teamed up with the Goblin King.

Menace rides a stolen Green Goblin glider.

WEB FILE

Menace uses weaponry and equipment stolen from the original Green Goblin, Norman Osborn. The Goblin serum gives her superhuman strength, stamina, speed and agility.

— POWER RATING —

Intelligence	●●●●●○○○○○
Strength	●●●●●○○○○○
Speed	●●●○○○○○○○
Durability	●●●●○○○○○○
Energy Projection	●●○○○○○○○○
Fighting Skill	●●●●○○○○○○

MEPHISTO

The demon Mephisto is a being of unimaginable power. While Aunt May lay dying from a gunshot wound, Peter Parker looked to his magical allies for help. When his efforts proved fruitless, Peter made a deal with Mephisto. In exchange for wiping Peter's marriage to Mary Jane from history, Mephisto restored Aunt May to health.

Mephisto is not satisfied with his underworld role, and wishes to control the lives of mortals.

Pulling the Strings

Mephisto agreed to erase the marriage of Peter and Mary Jane knowing that it would leave behind an echo of painful loss for Mephisto to enjoy for eternity. Mephisto's reality-warping abilities triggered a permanent change in the timeline, leaving no one with memories of Peter and Mary Jane's relationship.

If he wishes, Mephisto can disguise his true form.

The limits of Mephisto's powers are unknown.

"I will do anything for the sound of a soul in pain."

WEB FILE

Mephisto has limitless magical powers, strength, and stamina. He is immortal, can shapeshift, and possess the souls of those who willingly surrender them.

— POWER RATING —

Intelligence	●●●●●●○
Strength	●●●●●●○
Speed	●●●●●●○
Durability	●●●●●●○
Energy Projection	●●●●●○○
Fighting Skill	●●●●●○○

MESMERO

WEB FILE

Mesmero is the most powerful hypnotist on Earth, and can make others do whatever he wants with ease.

—— POWER RATING ——

Intelligence	●●●●○○○○○○
Strength	●●●○○○○○○○
Speed	●○●○○○○○○○
Durability	●●○○○○○○○○
Energy Projection	●●●●○○○○○○
Fighting Skill	●●●○○○○○○○

Mesmero made his name as a convincing stage hypnotist, but in truth he had been born with the power of mind control thanks to his mutant genetics. When Mesmero tried to hypnotize an audience into surrendering their valuables, he made a lifelong enemy of Spider-Man.

Making Enemies

Mesmero found an ally in Magneto, arch-foe of the X-Men, and committed himself to Magneto's goal of world domination by mutantkind. However, Mesmero still intrudes on Spidey's home turf whenever he wants to make a big score.

Though he has studied the science of hypnotism, most of Mesmero's talent is genetic.

"Spider-Man spoiled my revenge. But the last laugh will be mine!"

Mesmero's flaw is his overconfidence. He is so convinced that his hypnotism will work on anyone, he can be beaten by a strong-minded opponent.

Mesmero controls his enemies from afar, and therefore his costume doesn't need to offer much protection.

MILES MORALES

In a parallel universe, Spider-Man died battling the Green Goblin. Teenager Miles Morales, infected by a bite from a spider genetically enhanced with Norman Osborn's OZ formula, chose to follow in the footsteps of the late Peter Parker and become the Spider-Man of his world.

Miles's "spider-camouflage" can make him virtually invisible.

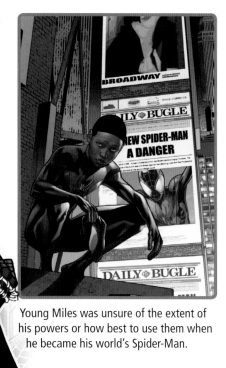

Young Miles was unsure of the extent of his powers or how best to use them when he became his world's Spider-Man.

Worlds Collide

The two Spider-Men met face-to-face when a dimensional rift brought Spider-Man into the alternate world inhabited by Miles Morales. Peter Parker recognized that Miles was only a teenager, but Miles's angry demands for information got the two heroes off on the wrong foot.

WEB FILE

Miles has Spider-Man's powers and more. He can paralyze foes with an electrically-charged "venom strike", and possesses "spider-camouflage".

— POWER RATING —

Intelligence	●●●●●○○
Strength	●●●●○○○
Speed	●●●●○○○
Durability	●●●○○○○
Energy Projection	●●●○○○○
Fighting Skill	●●●●●○○

MINDWORM

WEB FILE

Mindworm stole thoughts and emotions from others, nourishing himself, but ultimately causing his victims to die. He could also read minds, control others with his mind, and levitate.

— POWER RATING —

Intelligence	●●●●●○○○○○
Strength	●●○○○○○○○○
Speed	●●○○○○○○○○
Durability	●●●○○○○○○○
Energy Projection	●●●●○○○○○○
Fighting Skill	●●●○○○○○○○

William Turner, the boy who came to be known as Mindworm, discovered the horrifying extent of his mental powers when he accidentally killed his parents. He eventually settled in New York, secretly feeding on the emotions of the city's residents. After he tried to drain Peter Parker's thoughts, he bravely reconsidered his evil ways.

Oversized skull suggests tremendous mental powers.

A Tragic Fall

Sadly, Mindworm could not find a way to control his powers. After his release from prison he became a homeless vagrant. Despite his misery, Mindworm refused to use his powers to steal money or take revenge, still inspired by the heroic example of Spider-Man.

"I sense power, a strength of will—a mind seething with emotion!"

Mindworm was reduced to begging in the street.

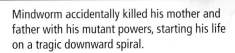
Mindworm accidentally killed his mother and father with his mutant powers, starting his life on a tragic downward spiral.

MIRAGE

One of the world's top specialists in the field of three-dimensional holograms, Desmond Charne decided to exploit his expertise by becoming the villainous Mirage. His costume incorporates miniature holographic projectors that can generate illusions and even turn him invisible – handy tricks when facing a foe as resourceful, agile, and strong as Spider-Man!

If Spider-Man can connect with a punch, he can knock out Mirage. The trick is finding the true target!

Spidey can be fooled into fighting a hologram of Mirage.

"I am called Mirage, and I've come here to rob you blind!"

Hoping for His Big Break
Mirage earned a bad reputation when he tried to rob the guests at Betty Brant and Ned Leeds' wedding. Spider-Man put him behind bars, and Mirage later died at the hands of an underworld vigilante. He has returned to life and serves as a member of the Hood's criminal army.

Costume fitted with holographic technology.

WEB FILE
Mirage projects holographs to help commit crimes with his gang. His gun fires tranquilizer darts as well as bullets.

— POWER RATING —
Intelligence ●●●●●○○○○○
Strength ●●●●○○○○○○
Speed ●●○○○○○○○○
Durability ●●●●○○○○○○
Energy Projection ●●●●○○○○○○
Fighting Skill ●●●●○○○○○○

MISS ARROW

A reborn Spider-Man emerged from a cocoon after a battle with Morlun, but the discarded husk of his old self came to life as his wicked opposite. This being called itself "The Other" and later went undercover as Miss Arrow, a nurse at Midtown High School. She hid her true nature while keeping an eye on fellow faculty member Peter Parker and waiting for her time to strike.

A Monster in Disguise

Miss Arrow developed an attraction to Flash Thompson, who was working at Midtown High School as a sports coach. When Flash refused to become her new host, Miss Arrow burst into thousands of spiders and attacked him. Spider-Man arrived just in time to end her threat.

Body can break into many smaller spiders.

WEB FILE

Miss Arrow could control and command the spiders that made up her body. She could also transform into a swarm of spiders. Spider-stingers on her wrists could inject venom.

— POWER RATING —

Intelligence	●●●●●○○○○○
Strength	●●●●○○○○○○
Speed	●●○○○○○○○○
Durability	●●●●○○○○○○
Energy Projection	●●○○○○○○○○
Fighting Skill	●●●●●○○○○○

"One lives... the other must die."

Once she dropped her convincing human disguise, Miss Arrow could use all of her spider powers against Spider-Man.

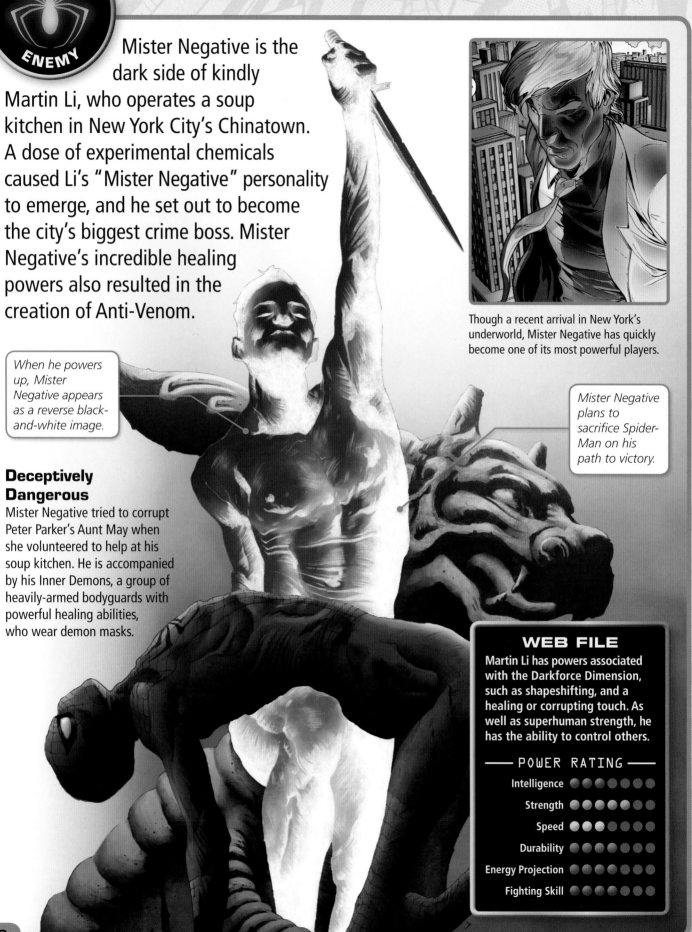

MISTER NEGATIVE

Mister Negative is the dark side of kindly Martin Li, who operates a soup kitchen in New York City's Chinatown. A dose of experimental chemicals caused Li's "Mister Negative" personality to emerge, and he set out to become the city's biggest crime boss. Mister Negative's incredible healing powers also resulted in the creation of Anti-Venom.

Though a recent arrival in New York's underworld, Mister Negative has quickly become one of its most powerful players.

When he powers up, Mister Negative appears as a reverse black-and-white image.

Mister Negative plans to sacrifice Spider-Man on his path to victory.

Deceptively Dangerous

Mister Negative tried to corrupt Peter Parker's Aunt May when she volunteered to help at his soup kitchen. He is accompanied by his Inner Demons, a group of heavily-armed bodyguards with powerful healing abilities, who wear demon masks.

WEB FILE

Martin Li has powers associated with the Darkforce Dimension, such as shapeshifting, and a healing or corrupting touch. As well as superhuman strength, he has the ability to control others.

— POWER RATING —

Intelligence	●●●●●●●
Strength	●●●●●●○
Speed	◐●●○○○○
Durability	●●●●●○○
Energy Projection	●●●●●●○
Fighting Skill	●●●●●●○

MOLTEN MAN

WEB FILE

Molten Man can slip from any grasp and has superhuman strength. He can make his body so hot that it can melt most materials. His slightest touch can cause severe burns.

— POWER RATING —

Intelligence ●●●●●○○○○○
Strength ●●●●●●○○○○
Speed ●●○○○○○○○○
Durability ●●●●○○○○○○
Energy Projection ●○○○○○○○○○
Fighting Skill ●●●●○○○○○○

An industrial accident left Mark Raxton coated from head to toe in a liquid metal alloy. He pursued a criminal career as the Molten Man, but his condition worsened until his metal skin grew so hot it threatened to burn him alive. His stepsister, Liz Allan, helped him, causing Mark to rediscover the value of human kindness.

The incredibly painful transformation into a being of burning metal made Mark Roxton a tragic figure.

Helping Where He Can

The Molten Man occasionally lends a hand to Spider-Man. However, he has difficulty controlling his emotions, and if he feels that his family members are in danger the Molten Man can become a boiling cauldron of white-hot rage.

The Molten Man throws punches that can melt iron.

"I'm burning alive, and you can all burn with me!"

MOON KNIGHT

SPIDEY STATUS
ALLY

Marc Spector was a soldier-for-hire, until an assignment in Egypt left him near death. Revived by the Egyptian god of vengeance Khonshu, Marc became Moon Knight. His personal fortune funds his crimefighting, and he carries an array of throwing blades and other specialty weapons. Moon Knight is one of Spider-Man's nocturnal allies.

His wealth allows Moon Knight to employ a large number of crime-fighting devices, including motorcycles and helicopters.

Moon Knight carries a wide variety of weapons, including pistols.

"If the law doesn't put you away permanently, the Moon Knight will!"

On his costume, Moon Knight bears the crescent moon symbol of Khonshu.

Multiple Personalities

Unlike Spider-Man, Moon Knight maintains more than one secret identity. As wealthy financier Steven Grant he mingles with high society, while he gets a street-level view of the action by posing as taxi driver Jake Lockley.

WEB FILE

Moon Knight wields various weapons given to him by the Egyptian god Khonshu. He has great strength and durability but his powers wax and wane with the phases of the moon.

— POWER RATING —

Intelligence	●●●●●●○
Strength	●●●●●○○
Speed	●●○○○○○
Durability	●●●●○○○
Energy Projection	●●○○○○○
Fighting Skill	●●●●●○○

MORBIUS

WEB FILE

Morbius has enhanced strength, speed, and senses, the powers of hypnosis and gliding, and sharp fangs and claws. He is a genius-level scientist.

— POWER RATING —

Intelligence
Strength
Speed
Durability
Energy Projection
Fighting Skill

Morbius has the fangs, the bloodlust, and the weakness to sunlight of a true vampire, but his powers don't have a supernatural origin. Transformed by an experimental blood serum, Dr. Michael Morbius contracted "pseudo-vampirism" to become Morbius, the Living Vampire! His greatest wish is to be rid of his condition forever.

Suspicious Minds

Morbius the Living Vampire secretly worked with Horizon Labs to create a cure for New York's spider-virus. He hoped this role might help him to find his own salvation, but instead he was met with hostility by government investigators when his identity was revealed.

Spider-Man tries to help Morbius, but the Living Vampire's killer instinct is strong.

When his heroic instincts win out, Morbius works to help the Super Hero community in their fight against evil forces.

MORLUN

Morlun has walked the Earth for centuries, feeding on the life forces of lesser beings while seeking out the pure energy of "totems," the human avatars of primal animal spirits. Believing Spider-Man to be the bearer of the spider totem, Morlun tracked him relentlessly, hoping to consume the spider's essence and prolong his own life.

WEB FILE
Morlun absorbs the life forces of other beings. His strength varies depending on how recently he has fed.

─ POWER RATING ─

Intelligence	●●●●●○○○
Strength	●●●●●●○○
Speed	●●●○○○○○
Durability	●●●●●○○○
Energy Projection	●●●●●○○○
Fighting Skill	●●●●●○○○

"Your time is near. Say your goodbyes."

Primal Predator
Spider-Man and the mysterious Ezekiel teamed up to defeat Morlun, seemingly wiping him from existence. But Morlun has returned from the dead several times since then, drawing on his connection to the spiritual energy of living beings to fuel his resurrections.

Morlun's old-fashioned attire indicates his age.

Morlun can seemingly appear and disappear at will.

Morlun came close to ending Spider-Man's life, but the web-swinger battled back from the brink of death to defeat his tormentor.

MS. MARVEL

WEB FILE

Ms. Marvel can fly and has superhuman strength, stamina, and durability. She can also absorb and rechannel energy.

— POWER RATING —

Intelligence ●●●●●○○○○○
Strength ●●●●●●○○○○
Speed ●○○○○○○○○○
Durability ●●●●●○○○○○
Energy Projection ●●●●●○○○○○
Fighting Skill ●●●●●●○○○○

Air Force veteran Carol Danvers has worked as a journalist and editor, but her most famous role is that of the Super Hero Ms. Marvel. While working for NASA, Danvers encountered the alien Kree Empire, and was turned into a half-Kree, superhuman hybrid. She later served with the New Avengers alongside her teammate Spider-Man.

Ms. Marvel's control of energy gives her an edge over other Super Heroes.

New Responsibilities

Carol is now known as Captain Marvel, and her new abilities have put her in the elite company of the most powerful heroes on Earth. She is at least the fourth person to hold the Captain Marvel title and has vowed to honour it through selflessness and bravery.

"We've got the advantage, Spider-Man— let's not throw it away!"

Spider-Man has known Ms. Marvel for years and the two work well together.

Control over electromagnetism allows Ms. Marvel to absorb energy and release it as destructive photon blasts.

MYSTERIO

Hollywood stuntman and special-effects whiz Quentin Beck learned that crime could pay after he quit his job and became the villain Mysterio. Whenever Spider-Man fights Mysterio, he has a tough time figuring out what's real and what's an illusion!

Helmet protects from smoke used to confuse opponents.

Though he tries to make it appear as if he has mystical powers, Mysterio relies on mind control and stagecraft tricks.

Unfinished Business

Mysterio originally wished to take Spider-Man's place as a Super Hero, until Spidey put a stop to his scheming. Mysterio later died, but seemingly returned from the afterlife to continue to vex Spider-Man. He worked for Sasha Kravinoff as part of a plot to bring her husband, Kraven the Hunter, back to the land of the living so that he could get revenge on Spider-Man.

Mysterio can conceal weapons beneath his cloak.

WEB FILE

Mysterio was once a leading movie special-effects designer, and uses his ability to create illusions to commit crimes and confuse Spider-Man. He is also a skilled hypnotist.

— POWER RATING —

Intelligence	●●●●●●●○
Strength	●●●○○○○
Speed	●●○○○○○
Durability	●●●○○○○
Energy Projection	●●●●○○○
Fighting Skill	●●●●○○○

NED LEEDS

Ned's will was dominated by the Hobgoblin.

Peter Parker and Ned worked together at *The Daily Bugle*, where Ned met and married secretary Betty Brant. Then Roderick Kingsley, the evil Hobgoblin, brainwashed Ned into acting as a decoy for his own activities. Criminals murdered Ned thinking he was the Hobgoblin, and Peter was determined to clear his dead friend's name.

"Spider-Man! How that name has haunted me."

In a rare moment of happiness, Ned married Betty Brant – only to have the villain Mirage interrupt the ceremony.

A Life of Hardship
A rival of Peter Parker's for the affections of Betty Brant, Ned won Betty's heart but later emerged as the primary suspect for the crimes committed by the Hogoblin. After Ned's death Peter proved his innocence, though many people still believed that Ned had lived a villainous double life.

WEB FILE
Ned was an experienced newspaper reporter. Under the influence of Roderick Kingsley he briefly used the Hobgoblin's weapons and equipment.

— POWER RATING —

Intelligence	●●●●●●○
Strength	●●●○○○○
Speed	●●○○○○○
Durability	●●●○○○○
Energy Projection	●●●○○○○
Fighting Skill	●●●○○○○

NICK FURY

Injured while fighting in World War II, Fury was saved by an injection of the Infinity Formula, which greatly extended his lifespan. He joined the C.I.A., working with Peter Parker's parents, Mary and Richard, and later became the director of S.H.I.E.L.D., the U.S.'s premier security agency. When Norman Osborn replaced S.H.I.E.L.D. with H.A.M.M.E.R., Fury formed the Secret Warriors.

Spymaster

Fury recruited Spider-Man and other heroes for a covert mission to Doctor Doom's home country of Latveria, hoping to overthrow the Latverian prime minister. The mission didn't go as planned, causing the heroes to grow suspicious of Fury.

Fury lost an eye during World War II.

"Nick Fury ain't watchin' the end o' the world in bed, Mister!"

Fury is an expert at most forms of unarmed combat.

Nick Fury goes into battle against terror with fellow Secret Warriors Dum Dum Dugan and Daisy Johnson.

WEB FILE

Fury is a highly experienced soldier, a superb military tactician, an expert with all kinds of weapons and at unarmed combat.

POWER RATING

Intelligence	●●●●●●●
Strength	●●●●○○○
Speed	●●○○○○○
Durability	●●●●○○○
Energy Projection	●●●○○○○
Fighting Skill	●●●●●●○

NIGHTMARE

When people fall asleep and start to dream, that's when Nightmare is at his most dangerous! He prowls an otherworldly dimension on his black steed Dreamstalker, gaining power from sleepers' nightmares and pushing dreamers further into fear and madness. Can Spider-Man defeat this nocturnal reign of terror?

"When I'm in control, dreams really can come true!"

In the dream realm, Nightmare has almost limitless powers. Spider-Man must face his worst fears to beat the demon.

Bad Dreams
Nightmare is the arch-enemy of the sorcerer Doctor Strange, but Spider-Man has also been pulled into the fight. During one of Spider-Man's early adventures, Nightmare tormented him with his most feared visions, including the exposure of his secret identity.

Dreamstalker carries Nightmare through the Dreamscape.

Spidey's spider-sense is no defense against Nightmare.

WEB FILE
Nightmare is a demon of great mystical power who usually targets victims when they are asleep. He can teleport.

— POWER RATING —

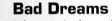

Intelligence	●●●●●●●
Strength	●●●●●●
Speed	●●●
Durability	●●●●●
Energy Projection	●●●●●
Fighting Skill	●●●●●

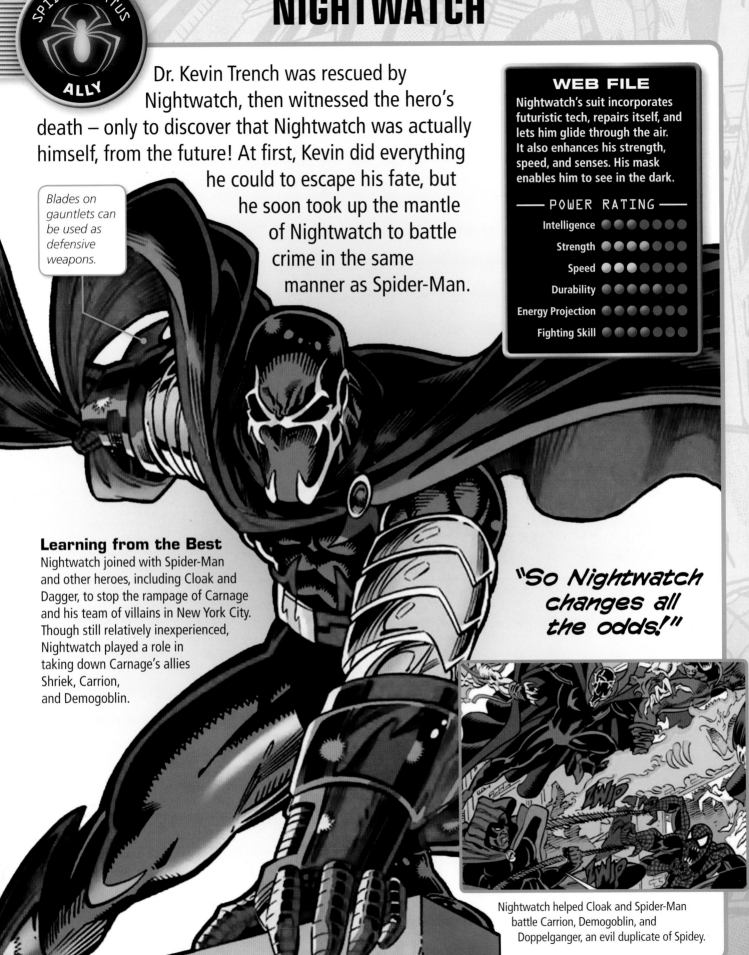

NIGHTWATCH

Dr. Kevin Trench was rescued by Nightwatch, then witnessed the hero's death – only to discover that Nightwatch was actually himself, from the future! At first, Kevin did everything he could to escape his fate, but he soon took up the mantle of Nightwatch to battle crime in the same manner as Spider-Man.

Blades on gauntlets can be used as defensive weapons.

WEB FILE
Nightwatch's suit incorporates futuristic tech, repairs itself, and lets him glide through the air. It also enhances his strength, speed, and senses. His mask enables him to see in the dark.

— POWER RATING —
Intelligence ⬤⬤⬤⬤⬤◯◯
Strength ⬤⬤⬤⬤◯◯◯
Speed ⬤⬤⬤◯◯◯◯
Durability ⬤⬤⬤◯◯◯◯
Energy Projection ⬤⬤⬤◯◯◯◯
Fighting Skill ⬤⬤⬤⬤◯◯◯

Learning from the Best
Nightwatch joined with Spider-Man and other heroes, including Cloak and Dagger, to stop the rampage of Carnage and his team of villains in New York City. Though still relatively inexperienced, Nightwatch played a role in taking down Carnage's allies Shriek, Carrion, and Demogoblin.

"So Nightwatch changes all the odds!"

Nightwatch helped Cloak and Spider-Man battle Carrion, Demogoblin, and Doppelganger, an evil duplicate of Spidey.

NORMAN OSBORN

Power-mad Norman Osborn committed more evil deeds in his own name than he ever did as the Green Goblin! With the global resources of Oscorp Industries at his disposal, Norman went underground after the Green Goblin's "death" to launch plots against Spider-Man, including the creation of Peter Parker clones.

Insane ambition has driven Norman Osborn to become one of the most powerful men on Earth.

New Heights, New Lows

Norman Osborn achieved success as leader of the Thunderbolts, a government-sanctioned team of reformed villains. This allowed him to become director of S.H.I.E.L.D. successor H.A.M.M.E.R. and founder of a new team, the Dark Avengers, while wearing his own suit of battle armor as the Iron Patriot. However, in time, Osborn's power-mad Green Goblin persona once again possessed him and he was removed from office in disgrace.

Spider-Man can't just outfight Norman, he has to outthink him, too.

"I know exactly where my enemies are at all times."

Spidey may capture Osborn, but the villain always escapes.

WEB FILE

Osborn's brilliant mind specializes in international business, battlefield tactics, and criminal psychology. The Green Goblin serum gives him enhanced strength and reflexes.

— POWER RATING —

Intelligence	●●●●●○
Strength	●●●●○○
Speed	●●●○○○
Durability	●●●○○○
Energy Projection	●●●○○○
Fighting Skill	●●●○○○

OUTLAWS

Reformed villains Sandman, the Prowler, Will O' The Wisp, Paladin, and Rocket Racer joined forces at Silver Sable's direction as the Outlaws. They also took their orders from Spider-Man and proved a remarkably effective crimefighting team when they all worked together.

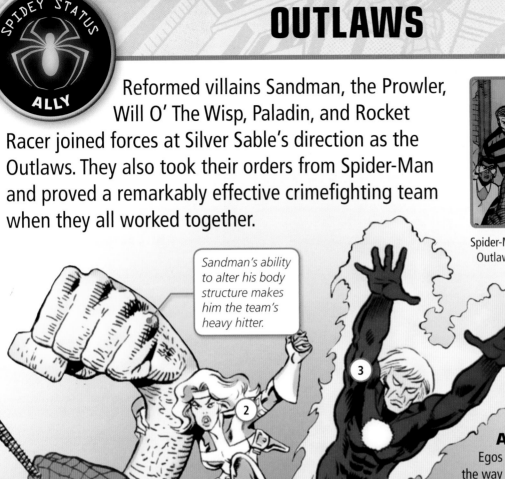

Spider-Man is the unofficial leader of the Outlaws, but sometimes finds it tough to get them all pulling in the same direction.

Sandman's ability to alter his body structure makes him the team's heavy hitter.

A Rocky Start

Egos and infighting sometimes got in the way whenever the Outlaws tried to work together during the early stages of a mission, but Silver Sable saw promise in her team. Exploiting the sometimes-greedy motivations of its members, she paid handsomely for successes.

Rocket Racer is the team's top speedster.

MEMBERS

1. **Sandman:** Control over his sand-like particles enables shapeshifting.

2. **Silver Sable:** Combat-trained mercenary.

3. **Will O' The Wisp:** Control over body density allows him to turn intangible and fly.

4. **Rocket Racer:** Uses rocket-powered gadgets and vehicles.

5. **Prowler:** Outfit incorporates climbing gear and weapons.

6. **Puma:** Mystical human-feline hybrid.

OVERDRIVE

WEB FILE

Overdrive disperses nanites which greatly enhance the performance of any ground vehicle while he is at the wheel. He is a skilled race-car driver and mechanic.

—— POWER RATING ——

Intelligence
Strength
Speed
Durability
Energy Projection
Fighting Skill

He claims to be Spider-Man's biggest fan, but Overdrive usually works against the wall-crawler when he's hired by crime bosses such as Mr. Negative. His ability to transform any motor vehicle comes in handy when Overdrive needs to flee the scene of his latest crime, but Spider-Man usually shows up to apply the brakes.

Upgrades can improve Overdrive's speed, armour, or weapons.

Driver in Demand

Overdrive recently signed up as one of the Sinister Six, modifying the gigantic Big Wheel to serve as the team's getaway vehicle. When Spider-Man disrupted the Big Wheel's gyroscopic balance unit, Overdrive's ride toppled uselessly on its side.

Overdrive instinctually knows how to drive his transformed vehicles.

If Spider-Man can get Overdrive out of the driver's seat, he can usually out-fight him and put the villain down for the count.

"Mind if I drive for a bit?"

123

PAPER DOLL

Piper Dali somehow survived a trip through a dimensional compressor, emerging as the two-dimensional villain Paper Doll. As Paper Doll, Piper became obsessed with the TV celebrity Bobby Carr, and murdered the people she considered his enemies, forcing Spider-Man to put a halt to her stalker behaviour.

Emotionally fragile and obsessed with celebrities.

WEB FILE

Paper Doll can make her body as thin as a piece of paper. She can stretch through tight spaces and slash with her razor-sharp edges, or even absorb victims, leaving only flattened bodies behind.

— POWER RATING —

Intelligence	●●●●○○○
Strength	●●●○○○○
Speed	●●○○○○○
Durability	●●●●●○○
Energy Projection	●●○○○○○
Fighting Skill	●●●●○○○

Lovesick and Lethal

Paper Doll also targeted the women who had dated Bobby Carr, ensuring that his affections would be directed at her alone. When Carr's latest girlfriend, Mary Jane Watson, landed in Paper Doll's sights, Spider-Man stepped in to save Mary Jane's life.

Able to become completely flat at will.

"You and I were meant to be together!"

In her two-dimensional form, Paper Doll can slip into any locked room to reach the object of her current obsession.

PALADIN

WEB FILE

Paladin wears a padded, bulletproof costume, carries a high-tech stun gun, and is a gifted combatant and investigator. He can also sense opponents before they attack.

── POWER RATING ──

Intelligence	●●●●●○○○○○
Strength	●●●●○○○○○○
Speed	●●●○○○○○○○
Durability	●●●●○○○○○○
Energy Projection	●●○○○○○○○○
Fighting Skill	●●●●●○○○○○

Paladin is quick to sing his own praises, but this mercenary has the skills to justify his high fee. His cases have sometimes brought him into partnership with Spider-Man, and Paladin has also worked as one of Silver Sable's Outlaws.

"No time to chat! It seems the next shift of guards has reported early!"

Ready to Assist

Spider-Man knows Paladin is reliable, as long as he gets paid. The two worked together to uncover a conspiracy that threatened to undermine Silver Sable's home nation of Symkaria. Paladin later joined the Thunderbolts, a team of reformed villains.

An armoured suit and plenty of weaponry keep Paladin ready for action.

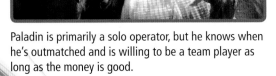

Paladin is primarily a solo operator, but he knows when he's outmatched and is willing to be a team player as long as the money is good.

PHALANX

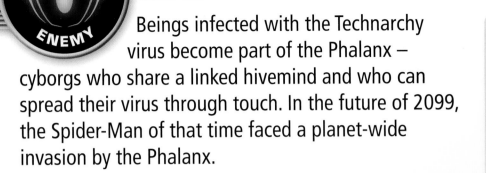

Beings infected with the Technarchy virus become part of the Phalanx — cyborgs who share a linked hivemind and who can spread their virus through touch. In the future of 2099, the Spider-Man of that time faced a planet-wide invasion by the Phalanx.

WEB FILE

The Phalanx can infect other beings with the transmode virus, making them cyborgs like themselves. They share their thoughts and have limited shapeshifting abilities.

— POWER RATING —

Intelligence	●●●●●●●○○○
Strength	●●●●●●●○○○
Speed	●●●○○○○○○○
Durability	●●●○○○○○○○
Energy Projection	●●○○○○○○○○
Fighting Skill	●●●●○○○○○○

Global Crisis

Only Spider-Man's alliance with Doctor Doom could halt the Technarchy virus. The future Earth of 2099 suffered greatly during the worldwide conflict known as the Phalanx War, but Spider-Man's courage helped bring an end to this devastating struggle.

Cybernetic sensor nodes allow the Phalanx to scan their victims.

Self-repairing components make each Phalanx member a tough opponent.

PROWLER

WEB FILE

The Prowler's costume incorporates dart shooters and gas canisters. He is a skilled martial artist and is a genius at inventing personal weaponry and hand-held gadgets.

— POWER RATING —

Intelligence	●●●●●○○○○○
Strength	●●●●○○○○○○
Speed	●●○○○○○○○○
Durability	●●●○○○○○○○
Energy Projection	●○○○○○○○○○
Fighting Skill	●●●●○○○○○○

Hobie Brown had an inventive mind but no money to get his ideas off the ground. He hoped to make his mark as the Prowler, using his day job as a window washer for inspiration. Spider-Man interfered with the Prowler's crimes, but he recognized that the newcomer had good intentions.

Reserve Hero

Inspired by Spider-Man's willingness to give him a second chance, the Prowler pledged himself to heroism. He later teamed up with other friends of Spider-Man as a member of the Outlaws. Prowler also occasionally helps Spidey develop new gadgets.

The Prowler's cape helps him blend into the shadows.

"Didn't expect me to have gas pellets in my boots, huh?"

Gas sprayers allow the Prowler to hide behind a smoke screen.

Talons assist in climbing walls and can also be used as weapons.

Spidey interrupted the Prowler's earliest crimes leading to a new destiny for the would-be cat burglar.

PUMA

Thomas Firehart is the Puma, ancestral champion of a Native American tribe. He possesses the supernatural ability to assume the form of a human-puma hybrid. He is also the CEO of Fireheart Enterprises, and briefly became the owner of *The Daily Bugle*. Puma and Spider-Man now help each other in the fight for justice.

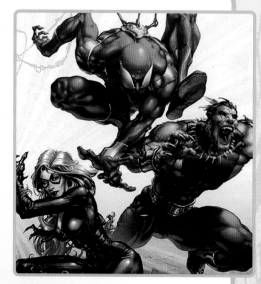

Sharp feline senses, especially smell, help the Puma sense danger.

Wearing his Iron Spider armour, Spider-Man teamed up with Puma and Black Cat to defeat the dinosaur villain Stegron.

Wealth and Honour

Although they originally met as adversaries, Puma and Spider-Man are now close allies. Both heroes have served on the same team, the Outlaws, working alongside reformed villains at the request of international mercenary Silver Sable.

"Claws or no claws, I'm still a gentleman..."

The Puma has thick muscles beneath his shaggy fur.

Extremely wealthy, the Puma can afford advanced electronic gear.

WEB FILE

Fireheart can transform into a werecat Puma, increasing in size and gaining enhanced senses of sight, smell, and hearing. He is highly trained in hand-to-hand combat techniques.

— POWER RATING —

Intelligence	●●●●●○○
Strength	●●●●○○○
Speed	●●●○○○○
Durability	●●●●○○○
Energy Projection	●○○○○○○
Fighting Skill	●●●●●○○

PUNISHER

WEB FILE

The Punisher is a deadly fighter, trained in unarmed combat and armed with a small arsenal of weapons including handguns, machine guns, grenades, and combat knives.

— POWER RATING —

Intelligence	●●●●●●○○
Strength	●●●●●○○○
Speed	●●○○○○○○
Durability	●●●●○○○○
Energy Projection	●●○○○○○○
Fighting Skill	●●●●●●○○

Military veteran Frank Castle's life changed forever when his wife and children lost their lives in a gang shootout. As the Punisher, he swore vengeance on his family's killers and organized crime. Spider-Man doesn't approve of the Punisher's methods, but the two often find themselves on the same side.

The skull insignia of the Punisher is feared by criminals worldwide.

"Take off, boy scout. This isn't in your wheelhouse."

Armed and Dangerous

Many of Spider-Man's most persistent enemies, including the Jackal and the Kingpin, have also launched plots to finish the Punisher once and for all. Even though Spidey and the Punisher have teamed up in the past to defeat their mutual foes, they wouldn't exactly call each other friends.

Spider-Man tries to minimize the collateral damage whenever the Punisher unloads on his enemies.

SPIDEY STATUS
ENEMY

Hoping to recreate more World War II super-soldiers like Captain America, the U.S. military experimented on Adriana Soria, transforming her into a humanoid spider. She became the Queen of all spiders, and pursued Spider-Man as her ideal mate. She believed that her power over the "insect gene" in Peter would enable her to make him do her will. Thwarted, the Queen later attempted to take over Manhattan.

Reborn as the titanic Spider Queen, Adriana briefly ruled over the people of New York City.

Defeating the Queen

Back during World War II, Adriana briefly dated Steve Rogers, better known as Captain America. However, Cap has fought at Spider-Man's side whenever the Queen has threatened New York City. And when the Queen later mutated Cap into a "Spider-King," Spidey was on hand to help restore Cap's humanity.

The super soldier serum has slowed the Queen's aging.

WEB FILE

Adriana can control anyone possessing the "insect gene." The super-soldier program has given her superhuman abilities. She also possesses a destructive sonic scream.

—— POWER RATING ——

Intelligence	●●●●●○○
Strength	●●●●○○○
Speed	●●○○○○○
Durability	●●●○○○○
Energy Projection	●●●●●○○
Fighting Skill	●●●●○○○

By not dressing for a battle, she confuses her foes.

RANDY ROBERTSON

WEB FILE

Randy has no superpowers, but is an excellent journalist and committed to whatever good cause he champions.

—— POWER RATING ——

Intelligence	●●●●●●●●●●
Strength	●●●●●●●●●●
Speed	●●◐●●●●●●●
Durability	●●●●●●●●●●
Energy Projection	●●●●●●●●●●
Fighting Skill	●●●●●●●●●●

Son of *The Daily Bugle*'s Robbie Robertson, Randy Robertson attended Empire State University along with Peter Parker. Known for his student activism and his courage in speaking up for the less fortunate, Randy pursued a career in social work. He and Peter were once roommates, and Randy is still a close friend.

"Buddy, you picked the wrong guy on the wrong day!"

Randy is a quick thinker with a stubborn streak.

Making His Way

In addition to social work, Randy has dabbled in acting and as a videographer for *The Daily Bugle*. During an outbreak of spider-powers across New York City caused by the Queen, Randy temporarily gained super-strength and the ability to stick to walls – until Spider-Man put an end to the Queen's bizarre and frightening reign.

Randy is often caught up in Spider-Man's adventures, but he doesn't know that Spidey is his friend Peter.

RAPTOR

Rewriting his own genetic code to include DNA derived from velociraptor dinosaurs, scientist Dr. Damon Ryder gained the ability to sprout claws and fangs as the superpowered Raptor. He blamed Peter Parker's clone Ben Reilly for the deaths of his wife and children, but misidentified the real Peter as the object of his vendetta.

Genetic tampering has given Dr. Ryder the fearsome fangs of a prehistoric predator.

Mistaken Identity

Raptor tracked the person he believed to be Ben Reilly to the home of Aunt May, forcing Peter Parker to prove to Raptor that he had the wrong man. Peter then forced Raptor to realize that he alone carried the responsibility for the death of his family.

Super strength makes Raptor a match for Spider-Man.

His armoured suit and an arsenal of weapons give Raptor additional advantages.

"I'm not letting you take this away from me!"

WEB FILE

A serum created from dinosaur DNA gives Raptor superhuman strength and stamina. His jaw can elongate and fill with sharp teeth, and he has retractable bone blades in his arms.

— POWER RATING —

Intelligence	●●●●●●●○
Strength	●●●●●○○
Speed	●●●○○○○
Durability	●●●●●○○
Energy Projection	●●●●○○○
Fighting Skill	●●●●●○○

RAZORBACK

Trucker Buford Hollis has the amazing gift of knowing how to drive anything—from a big rig to an alien spacecraft! Inspired by the exploits of costumed heroes like Spider-Man, he became Razorback, and later teamed up with Spidey while searching for his missing sister in New York.

In their first team-up, Spider-Man and Razorback saved each other's lives when threatened by an evil cult.

"Hold on to your lunches, good buddies!"

Spider-Man was surprised by Razorback's ability to take a punch.

Razorback is a talented wrestler.

Jumping in with Both Feet

When Razorback decided to join the Super Hero business, he modelled himself on the big-city heroes he'd heard about. This resulted in an all-out brawl between himself and Spider-Man, which Razorback considered a friendly way to introduce himself as the new kid on the block.

WEB FILE

Razorback's mutant power enables him to drive or pilot any kind of vehicle. He has superhuman strength and is an excellent hand-to-hand fighter, inventor, and mechanic.

—— POWER RATING ——

Intelligence	●●●●○○○
Strength	●●●●○○○
Speed	●●○○○○○
Durability	●●●○○○○
Energy Projection	●●○○○○○
Fighting Skill	●●●●○○○

REED RICHARDS

Genius Reed Richards designed the spacecraft for the mission that gave him and his companions super powers, and under the name Mister Fantastic he founded the Fantastic Four. Reed encourages Spider-Man's scientific curiosity as a Married to Sue Storm (Invisible Woman), Reed is also the father of Franklin and Valeria Richards.

Dr. Richards is often invited to receive awards for science.

Reed tries to avoid stretching when not in costume.

Reed Richards' knowledge has earned him a place among an elite group – whose members also include Iron Man and Doctor Strange – who work to shape Earth's future.

> "It isn't often I'm outmaneuvered by a man-made compound."

Boundless Knowledge

Reed Richards is an expert in almost every field. He sees Peter Parker as a worthy student of the sciences and encourages him in his studies. He is one of the few who knows Peter's secret identity as Spider-Man.

WEB FILE

Exposure to cosmic rays means that Reed can stretch his body into any shape. However his most amazing ability is his natural scientific genius.

— POWER RATING —

Intelligence	●●●●●●●
Strength	●●●○○○○
Speed	●●○○○○○
Durability	●●●○○○○
Energy Projection	●●○○○○○
Fighting Skill	●●●●○○○

RHINO

The Rhino knows he's not the smartest villain in town, and gets angry at the thought that people are laughing at him behind his back.

If the Rhino's headed toward you, get out of the way! Thug Aleksei Sytsevich became permanently bonded to a tough exoskeleton and went into business as an unstoppable enforcer. Not big in the brains department, Rhino sells his services to smarter villains who tell him what to do.

"Shouldn't have got in the way of my bank job, bug-boy!"

Spider-Man's best strategy is to stay out of the Rhino's reach.

WEB FILE

Gamma radiation gives Rhino superhuman strength, speed and durability. His powers are greatly enhanced by an armored polymer exoskeleton with the appearance of Rhino skin.

— POWER RATING —

Intelligence	●○○○○○○
Strength	●●●●●●○
Speed	●●○○○○○
Durability	●●●●●○○
Energy Projection	●○○○○○○
Fighting Skill	●●●●○○○

A Familiar Foe

Rhino has suffered a string of defeats trying to beat Spider-Man, but remains committed to the only life he has ever known. An experiment once gave Rhino a genius-level intellect, but he lost it just as suddenly.

ROBBIE ROBERTSON

One of the most respected staffers on *The Daily Bugle*, Joe "Robbie" Robertson helped Peter when he joined the staff of the newspaper as a photographer. For many years Robbie was a calm contrast to fiery Editor-in-Chief J. Jonah Jameson. He later became the paper's publisher.

Robbie was brave enough to stand up to J. Jonah Jameson's volcanic rages, and sometimes even made him see reason!

Past Secrets

For years Robbie was haunted by his failure to speak out against the hitman Tombstone. Spider-Man eventually helped him bring the killer to justice, and Robbie is proud to call Spidey his friend. Under Robbie's leadership, *The Daily Bugle* took a much more positive view of Spider-Man's heroics.

The Bugle's reporters know they'll be treated fairly under Robbie's leadership.

"The Bugle's run so many Spider-Man shots that he should be our official mascot!"

WEB FILE

Robbie is a newspaper editor, manager, and reporter of wisdom, courage, great integrity and intelligence.

— POWER RATING —

Intelligence	●●●●●●○
Strength	●●●○○○○
Speed	●●○○○○○
Durability	●●●○○○○
Energy Projection	●○○○○○○
Fighting Skill	●●●●○○○

ROCKET RACER

Inventor Robert Farrell turned to crime as Rocket Racer to support his family. Spider-Man helped him to follow a better path. After attending Empire State University, Rocket Racer joined Spider-Man's team, the Outlaws. Rocket Racer has since trained as hero at the Avengers Academy.

Now good friends, Rocket Racer and Spider-Man started off on opposite sides of the law.

Headset cybernetically controls Rocket Racer's skateboard.

Staying Straight

Rocket Racer has been tempted to return to the easy money of a criminal career, but has worked hard to provide for his sickly mother while staying on the straight and narrow. He briefly worked as an undercover S.H.I.E.L.D. operative.

"You're good, wall-crawler, real good. But the Rocket Racer is better!"

WEB FILE

Rocket Racer wears magnetic boots and rides a jet-powered skateboard. His gloves fire powerful mini-rockets.

— POWER RATING —

Intelligence	●●●●●○○○○○
Strength	●●●○○○○○○○
Speed	●●●●○○○○○○
Durability	●●○○○○○○○○
Energy Projection	●●●○○○○○○○
Fighting Skill	●●●○○○○○○○

RONIN

Ronin was one of Spider-Man's teammates on the New Avengers. But even her fellow Avengers didn't know Ronin's true identity! Maya Lopez eventually revealed herself as the masked hero. Other heroes know that her deafness doesn't stand in the way of her crime-fighting expertise.

Ronin prefers to use traditional Japanese weapons, such as *nunchaku* sticks connected by a chain or a *katana* sword.

Ronin is deaf but able to read lips and body language.

Padded armour offers protection from bladed weapons.

Ronin is a superb martial artist.

Saved From Evil

Maya grew up in the Kingpin's care, but rejected her adoptive father after learning of his criminal nature. After adventuring under the name of Echo, Maya became Ronin during a mission to Japan with the New Avengers. Evildoers brainwashed Maya into becoming their pawn, but Spider-Man and other heroes helped rescue her.

WEB FILE

Ronin can instantly learn any combat move after seeing it once. She is a world-class athlete and combatant and highly skilled with most types of weapons, particularly swords.

— POWER RATING —

Intelligence	●●●●●○○
Strength	●●●●○○○
Speed	●●○○○○○
Durability	●●●●○○○
Energy Projection	●○○○○○○
Fighting Skill	●●●●●●○

ROSE

WEB FILE

The Rose took after his father and became a cunning criminal mastermind. He was skilled with most types of firearms.

— POWER RATING —

Intelligence ●●●●●○○○

Strength ●●○○○○○○

Speed ●●○○○○○○

Durability ●●●○○○○○

Energy Projection ●○○○○○○○

Fighting Skill ●●●●○○○○

Richard Fisk, son of the criminal Kingpin, was torn between a desire to join his father's underworld empire or overthrow it. Richard took the identity of the Rose and launched several attempts to topple the family business. Starting a gang war as the "Blood Rose," Richard seemingly died at his mother's hands.

"The web-swinger is disrupting my operations. I have attempted to solve the problem."

Feuding Family

As the Rose, Richard Fisk wore a full-face mask to keep his identity a secret. He soon earned a reputation as an unflappable mastermind. One of his criminal money-spinning rackets, fixing football games, was rumbled by Spider-Man and revealed by *The Daily Bugle*.

The Rose didn't rise to his lofty criminal rank without eliminating a few rivals. He could be charming but was utterly ruthless.

The Rose is quick to fire, but Spidey is even quicker.

SANDMAN

Flint Marko escaped from prison and stumbled on an atomic testing facility. Exposure to radiation turned him into the Sandman. Now composed of living sand and able to shapeshift into any form, the Sandman fought Spider-Man on his own and as a member of the Sinister Six and the Frightful Four, before making peace with the wall-crawler.

Sandman can control every particle of his body.

Sandman and Spider-Man have worked together on occasion, and both have been members of the Outlaws crimefighting team.

"Look alive, webhead! The Sandman's comin'!"

Good Intentions
Sandman isn't a bad guy, but in the past he has been driven to rage over his failure to protect Keemia, a little girl he views as his daughter. He has tried to obtain custody of Keemia, and has worked against villains like Doctor Octopus when he thought their actions would put the girl in danger.

Punches have little effect on Sandman.

WEB FILE
Sandman can transform all or part of his body into sand-like particles, grow to vast size and become superhumanly strong. He can combine his particles into weapons, or shoot them at foes.

— POWER RATING —
Intelligence	●●●●●○○
Strength	●●●●●●○
Speed	●●○○○○○
Durability	●●●●●●○
Energy Projection	●●●○○○○
Fighting Skill	●●●●○○○

SASHA KRAVINOFF

The widow of Kraven the Hunter, Sasha Kravinoff blamed Spider-Man for her husband's death. Her vengeful scheme forced Spider-Man to battle his most dangerous enemies one after the other until he was exhausted, and culminated in a war that Sasha called the "Grim Hunt," after her dead son, Vladimir, alias Grim Hunter.

Sasha brought Kraven back from the grave, but he claimed all she had given him was a corrupt "un-life."

"Shall we nudge the players in a different direction?"

Ruthless Mastermind

Sasha gathered the surviving members of the Kravinoff family, including her daughter Ana and Kraven's villainous half-brother, the Chameleon, in the hope of resurrecting her lost love Kraven the Hunter. She also kidnapped Madame Web and Spider-Woman Mattie Franklin. Her ultimate goal was the death of Spider-Man!

A master of manipulation, Sasha is an implacable opponent.

WEB FILE

Sasha is a cunning criminal and killer who will stop at nothing to get her way. She is also a trained hunter and martial artist.

— POWER RATING —

Intelligence	●●●●●●●
Strength	●●●●
Speed	●●
Durability	●●●●
Energy Projection	●●●
Fighting Skill	●●●●●

SCARLET SPIDER

Roderick Kingsley, the Jackal, created a clone of Peter Parker hoping he would destroy the real Spider-Man. After learning the truth, the clone decided to live as "Ben Reilly" and become the hero Scarlet Spider. Peter and Ben became good friends and saw themselves as brothers. Peter was devastated when Ben seemingly died in a clash with the Green Goblin.

The Scarlet Spider was virtually identical to Spider-Man. Out of costume, Ben dyed his hair blond to be different from Peter.

For a time, Peter even believed that he might be the real clone!

"There has to be a Spider-Man out there. I'm just not sure which of us it should be!"

Ben wore a distinctive costume to differentiate himself from Spider-Man.

More than a Brother
Ben Reilly has the same memories as Peter, and at one point he adventured as the one true Spider-Man. But after Ben died stopping the Green Goblin's plot to bomb *The Daily Bugle* building, Peter honoured his memory by retaking the Spider-Man role.

WEB FILE
As a clone of Peter Parker, Ben had the same powers as Spidey. Impact webbing and stinger missiles with sedatives in his arsenal increased his Energy Projection rating.

POWER RATING
Intelligence	●●●●●○○
Strength	●●●●●○○
Speed	●●●○○○○
Durability	●●●●○○○
Energy Projection	●●●○○○○
Fighting Skill	●●●●●○○

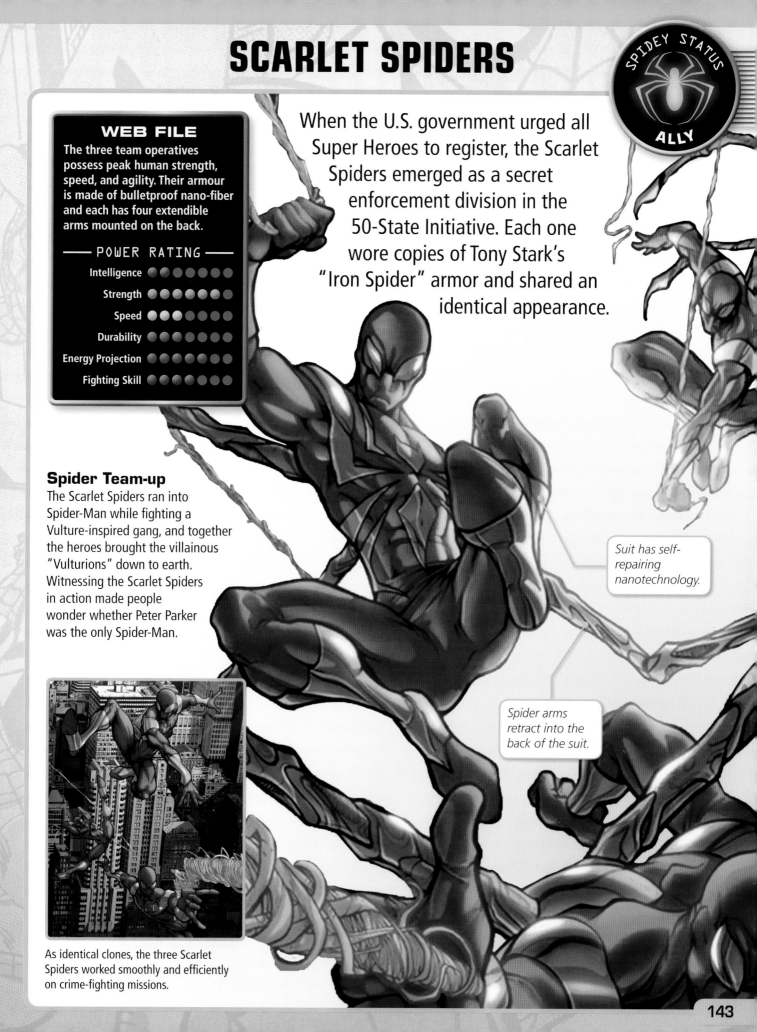

SCARLET SPIDERS

WEB FILE

The three team operatives possess peak human strength, speed, and agility. Their armour is made of bulletproof nano-fiber and each has four extendible arms mounted on the back.

— POWER RATING —

Intelligence ●●●●●○○○○○
Strength ●●●●●○○○○○
Speed ●●●○○○○○○○
Durability ●●●●○○○○○○
Energy Projection ●●●●●●○○○○
Fighting Skill ●●●●○○○○○○

When the U.S. government urged all Super Heroes to register, the Scarlet Spiders emerged as a secret enforcement division in the 50-State Initiative. Each one wore copies of Tony Stark's "Iron Spider" armor and shared an identical appearance.

Spider Team-up

The Scarlet Spiders ran into Spider-Man while fighting a Vulture-inspired gang, and together the heroes brought the villainous "Vulturions" down to earth. Witnessing the Scarlet Spiders in action made people wonder whether Peter Parker was the only Spider-Man.

Suit has self-repairing nanotechnology.

Spider arms retract into the back of the suit.

As identical clones, the three Scarlet Spiders worked smoothly and efficiently on crime-fighting missions.

SCORCHER

Furious when his boss accused him of stealing, chemist Steven Hudak built a suit armed with flamethrowers and, as the Scorcher, set out to burn the business to the ground. Spider-Man stopped the Scorcher, but the villain soon found his services in demand by crime bosses wanting to turn up the heat.

Heat blasts fired by Scorcher will cook Spidey to a crisp if he remains in the line of fire.

"You stick your nose in, you get it burned off!"

Flamethrowers are fed by fuel canisters built into the suit.

Scorcher's suit is completely fireproof – it has to be!

Hot Hire
Scorcher joined the Hood's criminal army to carry out raids against the Hood's rival, Mr. Negative. This gave Scorcher more opportunities to test himself against Spider-Man. The wall-crawler has proved too fast and agile so far, but Scorcher is determined to send Spidey up in flames.

WEB FILE
Scorcher's armored costume gives him superhuman durability and houses powerful flamethrowers. He flies using a jet pack.

— POWER RATING —
Intelligence	●●●●●○○
Strength	●●●●○○○
Speed	●●●○○○○
Durability	●●●●●○○
Energy Projection	●●●●●○○
Fighting Skill	●●●●○○○

SCORPION

WEB FILE

Scorpion has the strength and agility of a scorpion grown to human size. His battlesuit has a mechanical tail that can sting, fire electrical blasts, or rocket him into the air.

— POWER RATING —

Intelligence ●●●○○○○○○○
Strength ●●●●●○○○○○
Speed ●●●○○○○○○○
Durability ●●●●○○○○○○
Energy Projection ●●●●○○○○○○
Fighting Skill ●●●●○○○○○○

Transformed by an experimental mutagen, Mac Gargan gained the heightened strength and reflexes of a scorpion as well as a cybernetic battle suit with a quick-striking tail. J. Jonah Jameson ordered him to go up against Spider-Man, but the Scorpion couldn't strike a killing blow.

Trying Out a New Look

Mac Gargan later became the new host for the Venom symbiote, and even became a fake "Spider-Man" as a member of Norman Osborn's Dark Avengers team. But the Scorpion role was never far from his heart, and he soon returned to his classic identity.

Scorpion's tail is his most dangerous weapon.

"That's Scorpion, pal! The guy with the stainless-steel sting!"

Scorpion's suit is resistant to most attacks.

Different versions of Scorpion's battle armour have included built-in weapons and stabbing tail-tips, making him an unpredictable foe for Spider-Man.

SCREAM

This yellow-coloured alien symbiote bonded to security guard Donna Diego during an experiment orchestrated by the sinister Life Foundation. As Scream, Donna sought out Venom to help her control her form. Unfortunately, she lost her mind and began hunting down her fellow symbiotes.

Allies Becoming Enemies

Scream had good intentions when she bonded with her symbiote, believing that she and other hosts could use their powers to protect the planet. But her fluctuating mental state caused Scream to attack the others, which in turn made her a target.

Tendrils can grab and immobilize enemies.

Scream is unpredictable, switching between heroism, villainy, and insanity. When Scream appears, bystanders tend to run.

"The time for talking is over!"

WEB FILE

In Scream form, she can lash out at her enemies with the whip-like tendrils that extend from her head like strands of hair. She can also produce a deadly scream, called a Sonic Knife.

—— POWER RATING ——

Intelligence	●●●●●○○○○○
Strength	●●●●●○○○○○
Speed	●●●●●●○○○○
Durability	●●●●●○○○○○
Energy Projection	●●●●●○○○○○
Fighting Skill	●●●●●○○○○○

SCREWBALL

A new arrival on the villain scene, Screwball likes to show off with an elaborate routine of urban gymnastics and spectacular stunts. She makes sure that her exploits are live-streamed on the internet. When Screwball tried to masquerade as Spider-Man, her act came to a quick end when the *real* wall-crawler showed up.

Screwball's fearless gymnastic stunts can even keep her one step ahead of Spider-Man.

"This whole city's my playground!"

Publicity Hound
Screwball doesn't care if she gets money from her high-risk heists, as long as she gets on camera! She has a video crew operating the cameras that track her actions, uploading live footage to the internet and cutting compilation videos of her most outrageous stunts.

WEB FILE
Screwball has no superpowers, but is a superb gymnast and particularly skilled at leaping over rooftops.

— POWER RATING —
Intelligence	●●●●●●●
Strength	●●●●●●●
Speed	◐●●●●●●
Durability	●●●●●●●
Energy Projection	●●●●●●●
Fighting Skill	●●●●●●●

Screwball dives to avoid Spidey's web-shooter during a getaway.

Satchel contains recording equipment and spare batteries.

SCRIER

Scrier belonged to the mysterious Brotherhood of Scrier cult, answering to its chief, Norman Osborn. When the strange Judas Traveller manipulated Spider-Man and his clone Ben Reilly, Scrier stayed close at hand to ensure that everything unfolded according to Norman Osborn's wishes, before slipping back into the shadows.

Spider-Man fought the Brotherhood of Scrier, but its members are easily replaceable if one is defeated or captured.

"One does not question Mr. Osborn."

Dark Connections
Scrier gains his powers from the organization to which he belongs. The Brotherhood has deep ties to international businesses, the criminal underworld, and the political ruling class. The members of the Brotherhood seldom act directly, instead pulling strings from behind the scenes.

If forced to fight, Scrier makes a devious and dangerous enemy.

Scrier values stealth and prefers to operate from the shadows.

WEB FILE
Scrier is a cunning strategist and manipulator of others. He is also a formidable fighter, able to use an array of high-tech weaponry.

— POWER RATING —
Intelligence	●●●●●○○
Strength	●●●○○○○
Speed	●●○○○○○
Durability	●●●○○○○
Energy Projection	●○○○○○○
Fighting Skill	●●●●●○○

SENTRY

Robert Reynolds, alias the Sentry, is a powerful – and forgotten – hero. Years ago, in order to bury the dark side of his personality known as the Void, the Sentry erased the memories of his existence from every person on earth, including Spider-Man. He later enlisted in Norman Osborn's Dark Avengers.

Warring Natures

As a member of the New Avengers, Spider-Man fought alongside the Sentry but kept his distance from the man, knowing he was mentally unstable. The Sentry's evil nature, the Void, was on display most obviously during his time with the Dark Avengers and has resurfaced too often for Spider-Man to consider the Sentry a true hero.

"What I did— was it a good thing or a bad thing?"

The limits of Sentry's super-strength have never been tested.

WEB FILE

An advanced form of super-soldier serum gives Sentry the power of a million exploding suns. He can generate energy blasts and can even bring the dead back to life.

— POWER RATING —

Intelligence	●●●●●○○
Strength	●●●●●●●
Speed	●●●●●●○
Durability	●●●●●●●
Energy Projection	●●●●●●○
Fighting Skill	●●●●○○○

While serving with the Dark Avengers, Sentry gave in to the evil Void side of his nature and committed several serious crimes.

The villainous Shadrac is actually Dr. Gregory Herd, a genius who adopted the identity of Override and controlled machinery with a cybernetic headset – including Spider-Man's web-shooters! During an occult ceremony, he later received the supernatural gifts of Shadrac.

In a standoff with police, Shadrac simply laughed off the officers who threatened him with their handguns.

Too Hot To Handle

Spider-Man first tangled with Shadrac when he called himself Override. During their rematch, the villain had become a being of flame – a state that left him in constant pain. Spider-Man tried to ease Shadrac's suffering, but there appeared to be no cure for his blazing, burning condition.

"Bullets won't end my pain!"

With his body consumed by flames, Shadrac has a burning grip.

WEB FILE

Shadrac can summon and control flames, or manipulate the emotions of others to achieve whatever outcome he desires.

— POWER RATING —

Intelligence	●●●●●○○○○○
Strength	●●●●●○○○○○
Speed	●●○○○○○○○○
Durability	●●●●○○○○○○
Energy Projection	●●●●●●○○○○
Fighting Skill	●●●●○○○○○○

SHANG-CHI

WEB FILE

Martial arts training gives Shang-Chi amazing control over his body. He can ignore pain and resist drugs or poisons. His chi mastery gives him amazing strength and the ability to dodge bullets.

— POWER RATING —

Intelligence ●●●●●●○○○○
Strength ●●●●○○○○○○
Speed ●●○○○○○○○○
Durability ●●●○○○○○○○
Energy Projection ●○○○○○○○○○
Fighting Skill ●●●●●●○○○○

One of the best martial artists in the world, Shang-Chi is known as the Master of Kung Fu and a global champion for good. Tricked by his evil father into becoming an assassin, Shang-Chi rejected that path and worked to bring about his father's downfall instead. Shang-Chi trained Spider-Man in unarmed combat.

Shang-Chi studies the weaknesses of his opponents to know when best to strike.

Training Spider-Man

Shang-Chi agreed to customize Spider-Man's martial arts style to reflect the wall-crawler's superpowered speed and agility. Shang-Chi's special training gave Spidey an incredible edge when fighting his foes in hand-to-hand combat. The two heroes later teamed up against Mr. Negative, who was smuggling Chinese immigrants into the U.S.

Shang-Chi and Spider-Man make a formidable pair, combining combat mastery and superpowered agility.

A kick from Shang-Chi can knock out almost any villain.

SHATHRA

When Spider-Man met Ezekiel, he learned that he could be the mystical totem of the spider – a revelation that made him a target for Shathra, totem of the spider-wasp! Because spider-wasps are the natural predators of spiders, Shathra forced Spider-Man into a confrontation in which she revealed her true, deadly, insect form.

WEB FILE

Shathra is a Spider-Wasp with superhuman strength, speed, agility, and senses. She can teleport, has claws, and can fire sharp stingers.

POWER RATING

Intelligence	●●●○○○
Strength	●●●●○○
Speed	●●○○○○
Durability	●●●○○○
Energy Projection	●●●●○○
Fighting Skill	●●●●○○

Shathra can also take on a human form named Sharon Keller.

Forcing a Showdown

Guided by Ezekiel, Spider-Man arranged a rematch deep inside an African temple in order to turn the tables on Shathra. She lost their battle and became prey for the spider creatures that dwelled in the depths of the temple's catacombs.

"We are natural enemies. I will never go away."

Shathra's body is covered with sharp spines and stingers.

After luring Spider-Man into a trap, Shathra injected him with a numbing, paralyzing venom that nearly killed him.

S.H.I.E.L.D.

Formed after World War II as the Supreme Headquarters International Espionage and Law-Enforcement Division, S.H.I.E.L.D. is a global peacekeeping force that operates under a code of strict secrecy. S.H.I.E.L.D. is equipped with high-tech wonders, including a flying helicarrier, but at times has also been grateful for Spider-Man's help.

S.H.I.E.L.D. and its agents try to stay out of the public eye, but they provide support to more visible heroes like Captain America.

Nick Fury commands respect for his experience and leadership.

Under New Management

For a brief time, Norman Osborn replaced S.H.I.E.L.D. with his own sinister agency, H.A.M.M.E.R. When Osborn used the forces of H.A.M.M.E.R. to assault Asgard, the home of Thor, Spider-Man and other heroes worked to stop the war and discredit Osborn's organization.

MEMBERS

1. **Alexander Pierce:** Combat specialist and one of Nick Fury's chief lieutenants.

2. **Kate Neville:** Logistics expert and director of ordinance.

3. **Nick Fury:** Veteran soldier and frequent S.H.I.E.L.D. director.

4. **Al MacKenzie:** Multi-talented field agent with expertise in interrogation.

5. **The Contessa (Valentina de Fontaine):** Skilled undercover agent and weapons specialist.

SHOCKER

Safecracker Herman Schultz took his career to the next level by designing a pair of "vibro-smasher" gauntlets that released punches of energized air. He became the Shocker and preyed on armoured cars and bank vaults. Spider-Man has stopped him again and again, but the Shocker loves money too much to retire.

Padded suit absorbs any damage from his own blasts.

During an outbreak of a spider-virus in New York City, Shocker grew additional arms – making him twice the threat he was before!

Ready and Reliable

Shocker may not defeat Spider-Man often, but he has given the wall-crawler a run for his money. This makes Shocker a valuable criminal henchman, and he is often employed to delay Spider-Man and give another villain enough time to complete a crime.

"No one that lives can stand up to my twin punch!"

Shocker must brace himself before firing his vibro-smashers.

WEB FILE

Shocker is a gifted engineer who wears a protective, shock-absorbing battlesuit. His gauntlets have "vibro shock" units that project blasts of compressed air or destructive vibrations.

— POWER RATING —

Intelligence	●●●●●○○○○○
Strength	●●●○○○○○○○
Speed	●●○○○○○○○○
Durability	●●●●○○○○○○
Energy Projection	●●●●●○○○○○
Fighting Skill	●●●●○○○○○○

SHRIEK

When the alien symbiote Carnage broke out of prison, he took fellow inmate Shriek with him. Shriek can control soundwaves, allowing her to emit sonic blasts or manipulate the emotions and senses of her victims. Mentally unstable, she joined Carnage in his rampage across New York City.

WEB FILE

Shriek can generate a powerful sonic beam to use as a weapon or to fly. She possesses Dark Empathy, bringing out the bad side in people with her mind when her left eye shines.

— POWER RATING —

Intelligence ●●●●●○○○○○
Strength ●●●●○○○○○○
Speed ●●●○○○○○○○
Durability ●●●●○○○○○○
Energy Projection ●●●●●○○○○○
Fighting Skill ●●●●○○○○○○

Shriek can use her powers to induce fear and terror in people.

"Weaken with fear!"

Sonic Threats

Shriek doesn't care about innocents. When she teamed up with Carnage to attack the city, Spider-Man needed to work overtime to save New Yorkers from the physical damage and collapsing buildings triggered by her sonic screams.

Shriek seeks thrills at the expense of others, but has shown some affection for her fellow villains Carnage and Carrion.

SILVERMANE

Silvio "Silvermane" Manfredi is boss of one of the most powerful families in the Maggia crime syndicate and a perennial foe of Spider-man. Silvermane seemingly died during a battle with Dr. Barton Hamilton who had acquired the Green Goblin's powers. But Silvermane returned, with a cyborg body.

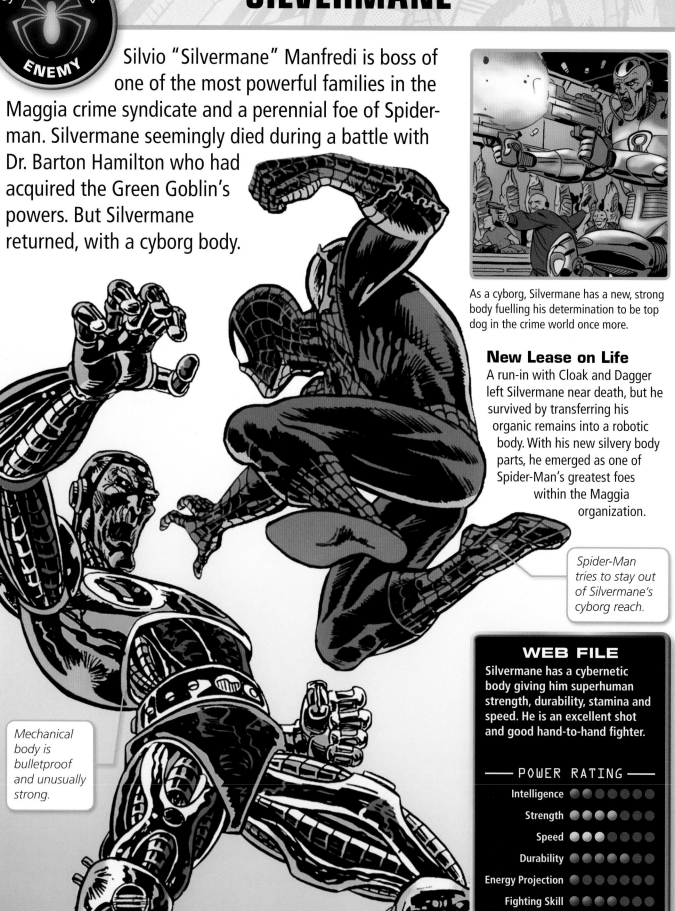

As a cyborg, Silvermane has a new, strong body fuelling his determination to be top dog in the crime world once more.

New Lease on Life

A run-in with Cloak and Dagger left Silvermane near death, but he survived by transferring his organic remains into a robotic body. With his new silvery body parts, he emerged as one of Spider-Man's greatest foes within the Maggia organization.

Spider-Man tries to stay out of Silvermane's cyborg reach.

Mechanical body is bulletproof and unusually strong.

WEB FILE

Silvermane has a cybernetic body giving him superhuman strength, durability, stamina and speed. He is an excellent shot and good hand-to-hand fighter.

— POWER RATING —

Intelligence	●●●●○○○○○○
Strength	●●●●○○○○○○
Speed	●●●○○○○○○○
Durability	●●●●○○○○○○
Energy Projection	●●○○○○○○○○
Fighting Skill	●●●●○○○○○○

SILVER SABLE

WEB FILE

Silver Sable is a superb martial artist, gymnast, hand-to-hand combatant, expert marksman and swordsman. She is also a fine leader.

POWER RATING

Intelligence ●●●●●○○○○○
Strength ●●○○○○○○○○
Speed ●●○○○○○○○○
Durability ●●●○○○○○○○
Energy Projection ●○○○○○○○○○
Fighting Skill ●●●●●○○○○○

Based in the tiny European country of Symkaria, Silver Sable commands a team of international mercenaries, the Wild Pack. Silver inherited the role from her father, who originally formed the Wild Pack to track down war criminals. She worked closely with Spider-Man when she formed the Outlaws.

Silver Sable has a number of operatives, but Spider-Man is one of her favourites.

Silver Sable is skilled with blades and firearms.

Silver Sable's protective costume does not hinder her natural agility.

"As long as you're working for me you'll obey my orders!"

Principled Leader

Silver Sable has high-paying clients, but only takes on assignments with aims she deems right and proper. Spider-Man believed that she died while helping him defeat Doctor Octopus and a new incarnation of the Sinister Six.

SIN-EATER

The mysterious Sin-Eater killed Spider-Man's friend, NYPD captain Jean DeWolff. A vengeful Spider-Man worked with police detective and former S.H.I.E.L.D. agent Stan Carter to solve her murder and those of other victims in the city – only to see Carter unmasked as the Sin-Eater!

Stan Carter wrongly believed he was acting for the greater good. After his arrest, he still had visions of his vigilante alter ego.

"Only those who have misused their power need fear the Sin-Eater's wrath!"

Suit conceals Sin-Eater's identity.

WEB FILE

Sin-Eater had police and government training and was an above-average combatant and detective. He had experience with a wide variety of firearms.

— POWER RATING —

Intelligence	●●●●●○○○○○
Strength	●●●●○○○○○○
Speed	●●○○○○○○○○
Durability	●●●●○○○○○○
Energy Projection	●●●●○○○○○○
Fighting Skill	●●●●●●○○○○

Hiding in Plain Sight

Stan Carter used his S.H.I.E.L.D. training to keep his true nature a secret from his fellow officers on the police force, while using case files to identify his next victims. He didn't target villains, but instead sought out authority figures that he judged had failed in their duties to the public.

Double-barrelled shotgun is Sin-Eater's favourite weapon.

SINISTER SIX

KEY MEMBERS

1. **Doctor Octopus:** Controls four mechanical arms.

2. **The Vulture:** Flies with a set of artificial wings.

3. **Electro:** Can generate destructive electrical bolts.

4. **Mysterio:** Able to generate illusions and hallucinations.

5. **Kraven the Hunter:** Physically strong hunter and tracker.

6. **Sandman:** Sand-like body can shapeshift.

Doctor Octopus formed the Sinister Six on one principle – strength in numbers! With Electro, Kraven the Hunter, the Vulture, Mysterio, and Sandman on his side, Doc Ock arranged a series of punishing attacks directed at Spider-Man in order to bring about Spidey's ultimate defeat.

"We must attack all at once! His power is not great enough to defeat all six of us!"

Enemies United

The Sinister Six have enjoyed a long life as a Super Villain team, even spawning a Sinister Seven and a Sinister Twelve! Through the team's various lineup changes, Doctor Octopus remained a key member, until he "died," and took over Spider-Man's body.

Mysterio's gloves and boots emit mind-bending gas.

Kraven wears skins from animals that he has killed.

SINISTER SYNDICATE

SPIDEY STATUS ENEMY

Taking inspiration from the Sinister Six, the Beetle recruited Hydro-Man, Boomerang, Speed Demon, the Rhino, and others to form a new villainous team, the Sinister Syndicate. They soon discovered that there was little honour among villains, and infighting – as well as Spider-Man – helped bring about the Syndicate's downfall.

Strength in Numbers

Unlike Doctor Octopus's Sinister Six, the Sinister Syndicate was more interested in profiting from crime than getting revenge on Spider-Man. They thought that their Super Villain team-up couldn't fail to make them super-rich, but they reckoned without Spidey.

Team leader Beetle is well-versed in attack strategies.

Rhino is the team's most powerful member.

Driven by greed, the Sinister Syndicate engaged in robberies and kidnappings. They didn't care who got hurt as long as they got results.

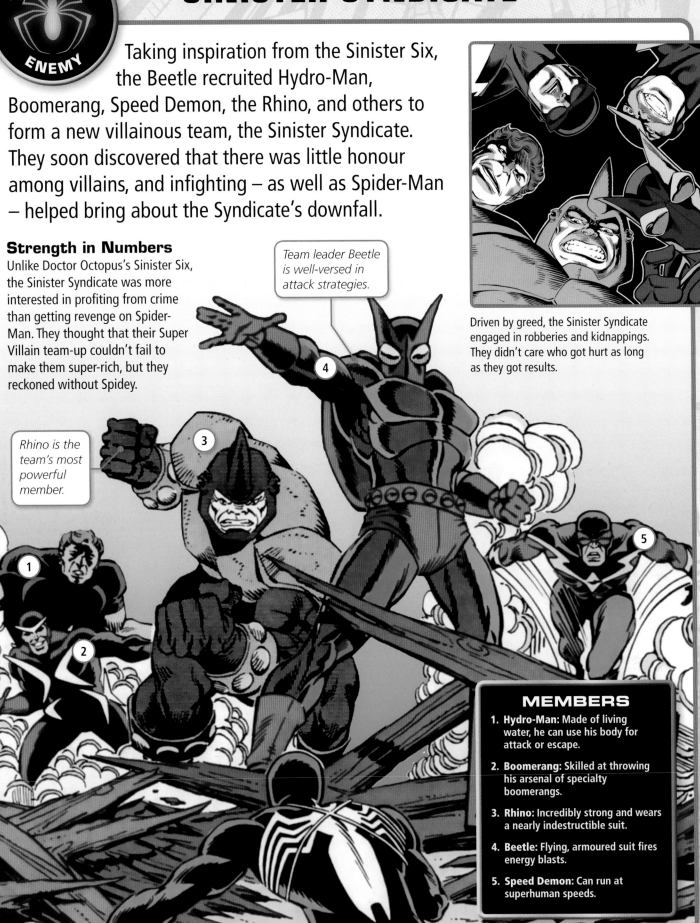

MEMBERS

1. **Hydro-Man:** Made of living water, he can use his body for attack or escape.

2. **Boomerang:** Skilled at throwing his arsenal of specialty boomerangs.

3. **Rhino:** Incredibly strong and wears a nearly indestructible suit.

4. **Beetle:** Flying, armoured suit fires energy blasts.

5. **Speed Demon:** Can run at superhuman speeds.

SLINGERS

Spider-Man created the alternate identities of Hornet, Ricochet, Dusk, and Prodigy for himself, but when he returned to his original role it fell to four teenagers to inherit Spider-Man's old costumes. As the Slingers, the rookie squad fought evil and tried to live up to the example set by Spider-Man.

Led by Prodigy, the Slingers had a rocky start, but grew to trust one another. They now work well as a team.

Dusk's powers are believed to originate from an alternate dimension.

Keeping the Faith

Before they could work together as a team, the Slingers needed to overcome their suspicions and learn to trust one another. They found a benefactor in the Black Marvel, a retired Super Hero who believed that the Slingers could follow in Spider-Man's footsteps and become heroes for the next generation.

MEMBERS

1. **Hornet:** Suit allows him to fly and can fire energy beams.

2. **Prodigy:** Suit provides damage resistance and enhanced strength.

3. **Dusk:** Can teleport and form solid constructs made of dark energy.

4. **Ricochet:** Superhuman agility and the ability to sense danger.

SLYDE

Discovering that he had invented a completely frictionless substance, chemist Jalome Beacher coated a costume with the stuff and became the slippery criminal Slyde. The costume allows Slyde to easily escape from Spider-Man's sticky webbing.

Slippery as an Eel

Slyde has a lighthearted attitude towards crime, convinced that his anti-friction technology will allow him to stay one step ahead of the police. Spider-Man has been forced to change his approach when dealing with Slyde, lest the inventive crook use his powers to slip through Spidey's fingers.

As he got better at using his suit, Slyde introduced new weapons to his arsenal, including swords and throwing stars.

"Make way for Slyde!"

Slyde's costume is completely frictionless.

Knee pads protect from hard landings.

WEB FILE

Former chemical engineer Slyde wears a costume covered with a substance so slippery he can slip through virtually any grasp. He can glide across any surface like he's skating on a frozen lake.

— POWER RATING —

Intelligence	●●●●●○○
Strength	●●●○○○○
Speed	●●○○○○○
Durability	●●○○○○○
Energy Projection	●○○○○○○
Fighting Skill	●●●●○○○

SOLO

SPIDEY STATUS
ALLY

WEB FILE

Solo has Special Forces training in counter-terrorism, and is an expert with various weapons and in forms of hand-to-hand combat. Cybernetic chips in his neck enable him to teleport.

POWER RATING

Intelligence	●●●●●●○○○○
Strength	●●●○○○○○○○
Speed	●●○○○○○○○○
Durability	●●●○○○○○○○
Energy Projection	●●○○○○○○○○
Fighting Skill	●●●●●●○○○○

The independent agent Solo is dedicated to the elimination of international terrorism. Armed and dangerous, Solo also has the ability to teleport directly into combat situations to get the drop on his foes. Solo notably teamed up with Spider-Man to defeat the Sinister Six.

"While I live, terror dies!"

Night-vision goggles for surveillance and targeting.

Man With a Mission

Solo has rejected his U.S. citizenship so that he can become a truly global force in the fight against terror. He has been a frequent ally of both Spider-Man and the Black Cat, and has lent his services to Nick Fury and the forces of S.H.I.E.L.D.

Armour has light-refractive properties for camouflage.

Solo's greatest weapon is his power of teleportation. He can teleport to safety while leaving a grenade behind for his enemies.

SPEED DEMON

Originally known as the Whizzer, Speed Demon is an old foe of the Avengers who fought Spider-Man while serving with one of the lineups of the Sinister Syndicate. Speed Demon moves so fast he can generate miniature whirlwinds with his body and knock down attackers.

It can be tough for opponents to hit Speed Demon, but he is weak against broad-range attacks like Shocker's blasts.

Pushing the Limit

His frequent defeats at the hands of Spider-Man led Speed Demon to join the team of villains-turned-heroes known as the Thunderbolts. While serving with the Thunderbolts, Speed Demon secretly made money on the side, committing crimes under his Whizzer identity.

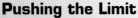

Agile and strong, Speed Demon fights best at super-speed.

Costume reduces friction at high speeds.

"Fame and fortune. I'm fast enough to take both!"

WEB FILE

Speed Demon has superhuman strength, stamina and durability, but his most notable attribute is his amazing speed. He is also a good hand-to-hand fighter.

POWER RATING

Intelligence	●●●○○○○
Strength	●●●○○○○
Speed	●●●●○○○
Durability	●●○○○○○
Energy Projection	●○○○○○○
Fighting Skill	●●●○○○○

SPIDEY STATUS ENEMY

SPENCER SMYTHE

WEB FILE

Smythe had no superpowers but is an engineering and robotics genius, who tragically used his great gifts for evil purposes.

— POWER RATING —

Intelligence

Strength

Speed

Durability

Energy Projection

Fighting Skill

Scientist Spencer Smythe created a robot called a Spider-Slayer to bring down Spider-Man and persuaded *Daily Bugle* editor J. Jonah Jameson to use it in a press campaign against the wall-crawler. Spencer's obsession with destroying Spidey led him to create more Spider-Slayers with different powers, but he never managed to achieve his dream.

"You seem surprised, web-slinger! I swore I would one day destroy you!"

An elderly man, Spencer was no match for Spidey in a fair fight.

The Smythe Legacy

Spencer Smythe died due to exposure to radioactive materials used in the construction of the Spider-Slayer robots. Even though he brought about his own demise, Spencer blamed his sickness on others. His son Alistair took up his father's vendetta and continued the construction of Spider-Slayer robots.

Each generation of Smythe's Spider-Slayer robots gained new ways to fight Spider-Man. The wall-crawler was surprised at first, but always won in the end.

SPIDERCIDE

One of the rejected clones of Peter Parker grown by the Jackal, Spidercide has a protoplasmic structure that allows him to shapeshift into different forms and which provides an astonishing resistance to damage. Spidercide betrayed the Jackal on the orders of his true master, Scrier.

Wisecracking Killer

Spidercide relishes his role as a nearly indestructible fighter – making jokes even after his head has been removed! He knows he is a clone and is happy to eliminate other clones, such as Ben Reilly, on the orders of his masters.

Spidercide has no conscience about using his powers to the max, especially when his opponent is Ben Reilly.

Shapeshifting allows for near-instant healing from any injury.

Super-strong punches can pulverize concrete.

"I like my programming! I'm daddy's boy all the way!"

WEB FILE

Spidercide is a clone of Peter Parker and has superhuman powers similar to Spider-Man, including spider-sense and wall-crawling.

— POWER RATING —

Intelligence	●●●●●●○○
Strength	●●●●●○○○
Speed	●●○○○○○○
Durability	●●●●●●○○
Energy Projection	●●●●○○○○
Fighting Skill	●●●●●○○○

SPIDER-GIRL ANYA CORAZON

WEB FILE

A magical, spider-shaped tattoo gives Anya powers similar to Spider-Man. She can generate her own webs from glands in her arms. She has received combat training from S.H.I.E.L.D.

—— POWER RATING ——

Intelligence ●●●●●●○○○○
Strength ●●●●○○○○○○
Speed ●●●○○○○○○○
Durability ●●●●○○○○○○
Energy Projection ●○○○○○○○○○
Fighting Skill ●●●●●○○○○○

Anya Corazon gained mystic abilities when the Spider Society chose her as their hunter and charged her with the responsibility of battling the Society's enemies in the Sisterhood of the Wasp. Anya later rejected the Spider Society and the name it had given her, Araña, to become the first hero to take the name Spider-Girl.

Earning Her Name

After enduring an ordeal in which Charlotte Witter stole the abilities of every spider-powered woman, Anya emerged with a new costume and identity. As she learned what it took to live up to the name Spider-Girl, Anya sought advice from other heroes.

"Why don't you stop acting like a chicken and face me already?"

Anya is adept at hiding in the shadows to surprise villains.

Anya is proud to wear the spider symbol.

As Spider-Girl, Anya soon became a fixture in the New York Super Hero scene, and sometimes teamed up with Spider-Man.

SPIDER-GIRL

In a future timeline, the daughter of Peter Parker and Mary Jane Watson carries on the family legacy as Spider-Girl! With her injured father retired from the dangerous business of crimefighting, May "Mayday" Parker secretly fights second-generation spider-villains while trying to live the life of a normal teenager.

In a near-future timeline, Spider-Girl swings freely though New York City.

Spider-Girl wears the same mask that her father made famous.

Her Own Hero

May Parker developed her powers at age 15. In her time as Spider-Girl she has fought a new Green Goblin – the grandson of the original – as well as battling Carnage after the alien symbiote attached itself to one of May's high school friends.

May wears her Spider-Girl costume under her school clothes in case adventure calls.

"You made a big mistake, fella!"

WEB FILE

As Peter Parker's daughter, May has superhuman strength, agility stamina, and durability similar to Spider-Man.

— POWER RATING —

Intelligence	●●●○○○○
Strength	●●●●○○○
Speed	●●○○○○○
Durability	●●●○○○○
Energy Projection	●●○○○○○
Fighting Skill	●●●●○○○

SPIDER-MAN 2099

In the distant future of 2099, scientist Miguel O'Hara gained superpowers, including the ability to scale walls with his finger-talons and a venomous bite. Inspired by the Spider-Man he had seen in historical records, Miguel donned a similar costume to battle villains as the Spider-Man of his era.

The Spider-Man of 2099 had a rocky run-in with the Spider-Man of the modern era during a time-travel adventure.

"This is fate, destiny! But I know how to change it!"

Barbs in fingertips are used for wall-crawling.

Streamlined costume allows for fluid movements.

WEB FILE

A laboratory accident gave Miguel similar powers to Spider-Man. He also has fangs and razor-sharp claws, and can move so fast he leaves a body double behind, confusing foes.

— POWER RATING —

Intelligence	●●●●●○
Strength	●●●●○○
Speed	●●●●●○
Durability	●●●○○○
Energy Projection	●○○○○○
Fighting Skill	●●●○○○

The Spider-Man of 2099 shares his predecessor's speed and agility.

Future Shock

In order to prevent his timeline from being erased, the Spider-Man of 2099 travelled backward in history, teaming up with the Spider-Man of the present day. His mission? To protect the life of his own grandfather, and make sure that Miguel O'Hara is born on schedule!

SPIDER-MAN REVENGE SQUAD

Gibbon, the Grizzly, the Kangaroo, and the Spot couldn't beat Spider-Man on their own – and their luck didn't change when they teamed up! They called themselves the Spider-Man Revenge Squad, but they were known as the Legion of Losers until, out of kindness, Spider-Man finally let them win.

"Maybe this revenge thing ain't all it's cracked up to be!"

Losing his battle suit doesn't stop the Kangaroo.

Infighting
The members of the team couldn't agree on what they wanted out of the Spider-Man Revenge Squad. Gibbon hoped to steer its members toward helpful heroism, but the vengeful Kangaroo only wanted to get the better of Spidey. The four teammates quickly came to blows.

Spot has the most powerful abilities on the team.

MEMBERS

1. **Kangaroo:** Armoured battlesuit allows for incredible jumps.

2. **Spot:** Can teleport himself or others via the spots on his body

3. **Gibbon:** Ape-like agility, strength and fighting skills.

4. **Grizzly:** Superhuman strength, stamina and durability, as well as razor-sharp claws and fangs.

SPIDER-SLAYERS

Built by Spencer Smythe and later by his son Alistair, Spider-Slayer robots come in all shapes and sizes and are programmed to hunt, capture, and destroy Spider-Man. Most Spider-Slayers have smooth surfaces that resist Spider-Man's webbing and can fire sticky webs of their own.

Advanced models of Spider-Slayers incorporate self-repairing metals and nanotechnology.

Upgraded
Spencer and Alistair also built Spider-Slayers that could be piloted by human operators, to give themselves a ringside seat for what they believed would be the final defeat of Spider-Man. Time after time Spider-Man overcame their fearsome technological know-how.

This robot can be remote-controlled or operated by a human pilot.

Spider-Man's powers are copied by the Spider-Slayer robots.

WEB FILE
The capabilities and power ratings of Spider-Slayer robots vary depending on the model, however, most possess web-shooters, the ability to scale walls, dangerous cutting blades and other weapons, and an anti-stick coating.

SPIDER-WOMAN JESSICA DREW

The first Spider-Woman started out as an agent of the sinister Hydra organization before devoting herself to heroism. In her civilian identity, Jessica Drew worked as a private investigator. Her unique Spider-Woman powers included the ability to fire electrical "venom blasts."

Jessica Drew's venom blasts are a potent offensive weapon against nearby enemies.

"You can try stopping me, but it won't be as easy as you may think."

Spider-Man and Spider-Woman have a long history of fighting side by side.

Who is the True Spider-Woman?

Jessica fell victim to the Skrulls, a species of alien shape-changers, who imprisoned her and impersonated her as Spider-Woman within the ranks of the New Avengers. When she escaped, she had to work overtime to regain the trust of her teammates.

Jessica's costume has a distinctive red-and-yellow pattern.

WEB FILE

A life-saving serum made from rare spiders gave Jessica abilities similar to Spider-Man. Trained in armed and unarmed combat, she can discharge venom blasts from her hands and fly.

— POWER RATING —

Intelligence	●●●●●○○
Strength	●●●●○○○
Speed	●●●○○○○
Durability	●●●●○○○
Energy Projection	●●●●○○○
Fighting Skill	●●●●○○○

SPIDER-WOMAN JULIA CARPENTER

WEB FILE

Julia Carpenter had superhuman strength, speed, stamina, and senses, and could wall-crawl like Spider-Man. She could create psi-webs with her mind and later gained the gift of future sight.

— POWER RATING —

Intelligence ●●●●○○○○○○

Strength ●●●●●○○○○○

Speed ●●●○○○○○○○

Durability ●●●●○○○○○○

Energy Projection ●●○○○○○○○○

Fighting Skill ●●●●●○○○○○

The second person to go by the name of Spider-Woman, Julia Carpenter was a government test subject who struck out on her own to become a Super Hero. In addition to her spider-powers, she can spin a "psi-web" of pure energy. Julia has also gone by the aliases of Arachne and Madame Web.

At one point, Julia Carpenter gave up being a Super Hero to look after her daughter, Rachel.

Spider-Woman's psi-webs can create barriers or catch people as they fall.

"Forget it, chump! You're not the only super-strong one around here!"

Big Changes

After Julia Carpenter gained the future-sight powers of Madame Web, she became an even bigger presence in Spider-Man's life. When Spidey temporarily lost his spider-sense ability, Julia stepped in to help him foresee major events that could threaten his loved ones.

SPIDER-WOMAN MATTIE FRANKLIN

Spider-Woman Mattie Franklin had the unique ability to sprout powerful spider legs from her back. Her promising career as Spider-Woman was cut short when the heirs of Kraven the Hunter set a trap for her, but Mattie may yet return.

Mattie had a playful, flirty character, as Peter Parker has occasionally discovered.

Mattie was capable of limited bursts of flight.

Sharp tips to her legs helped to grip slippery surfaces.

Speed and agility were two of Spider-Woman's greatest gifts.

Mattie's Final Battle

Mattie gained her powers during a mystic ceremony known as the Gathering of the Five. She seemingly lost her life in a similar ceremony, when the the villainous Sasha Kravinoff determined that her sacrifice would allow Sasha's husband, Kraven the Hunter, to walk the Earth once more.

WEB FILE

Mattie's superhuman strength, reflexes, and durability were magic-based. She also briefly absorbed the powers of others who had donned the mantle of Spider-Woman.

— POWER RATING —

Intelligence	●●●●○○○
Strength	●●●●●○○
Speed	●●●○○○○
Durability	●●●●○○○
Energy Projection	●●○○○○○
Fighting Skill	●●●●○○○

SPOT

Spot makes use of his teleportation portals during combat and turns Spidey's punch on himself.

Each teleporting spot can be detached and placed on a surface.

While researching teleportation technology for the Kingpin, scientist Jonathan Ohnn discovered how to create movable space-warp portals. By carrying the portals on his costume as the Spot, he leaped into a life of crime. When the Spot places his spots around a target, he can attack from many directions at once.

Target: Spider-Man
The Spot is usually a loner, but he joined with other villains as a member of the short-lived Spider-Man Revenge Squad. Spot's original goal was to gain cash from robbery, but long exposure to the strange energies given off by his teleportation portals has begun to damage his sanity, making his motives hard to predict.

WEB FILE

A lab experiment projected Jonathan Ohnn into the Spotworld dimension. He emerged as its living embodiment, the spots on his body dimensional portals.

— POWER RATING —

Intelligence ●●●●●○○○○○
Strength ●●○○○○○○○○
Speed ●●○○○○○○○○
Durability ●●●○○○○○○○
Energy Projection ●●●●○○○○○○
Fighting Skill ●●●●○○○○○○

SQUID

Thug Don Callahan underwent treatments that allowed him to transform at will into a tentacled, humanoid squid. As the Squid, he sold his services to local crime bosses, and encountered Spider-Man. The Squid lurks in sewers and, when cornered, has a variety of squid defences.

Hired Thug

Spider-Man doesn't take the Squid very seriously. During their first meeting, Spidey dismissed the new villain for his animal-themed gimmick and his ink-squirting powers. The Squid has tried to earn respect ever since.

The Squid's powerful, crushing tentacles are tricky to escape – even for Spider-Man.

Slippery, flexible body is difficult to damage.

WEB FILE

The Squid is able to shift from human form to squid form. His super-strong tentacles are used for attack, and his ink spray is a defensive weapon.

— POWER RATING —

Intelligence	●●●●●○○○○
Strength	●●●●○○○○○
Speed	●●○○○○○○○
Durability	●●●●○○○○○
Energy Projection	●●●○○○○○○
Fighting Skill	●●●●●○○○○

STEEL SPIDER

Teenager Ollie Osnick idolized Doctor Octopus so much he built his own mechanical tentacles. A close encounter with Spider-Man convinced Ollie to switch his loyalties. He redesigned the tentacles to resemble spider legs and became Spider-Kid, eventually settling for the identity of the Steel Spider.

WEB FILE

A brilliant engineer, Osnick designed his own mechanical limbs that resemble spider legs. He uses them for fast movement and as weapons.

— POWER RATING —

Intelligence	●●●●●●○○○○
Strength	●●●●○○○○○○
Speed	●●○○○○○○○○
Durability	●●●●○○○○○○
Energy Projection	●●●●○○○○○○
Fighting Skill	●●●●○○○○○○

Role Models

Ollie originally believed Doctor Octopus to be a misunderstood genius, not a true villain. Once he learned the extent of Doc Ock's criminal nature, Ollie realized that he didn't have as much in common with the mad scientist as he thought. Luckily, Spider-Man became the new object of his hero worship.

"I don't need you! You're all irrelevant! I don't need anyone at all!"

Each leg responds to Steel Spider's mental commands.

A control panel gives Steel Spider access to advanced functions.

Since his teenage years, Ollie has improved upon his original design. The Steel Spider legs allow him to scale walls and pin enemies.

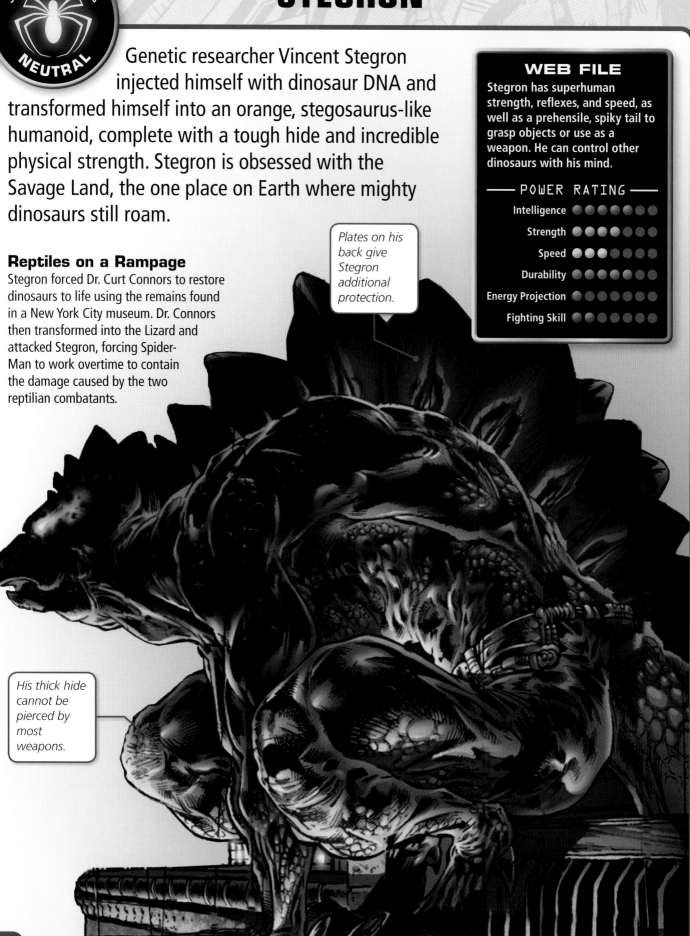

STEGRON

Genetic researcher Vincent Stegron injected himself with dinosaur DNA and transformed himself into an orange, stegosaurus-like humanoid, complete with a tough hide and incredible physical strength. Stegron is obsessed with the Savage Land, the one place on Earth where mighty dinosaurs still roam.

WEB FILE

Stegron has superhuman strength, reflexes, and speed, as well as a prehensile, spiky tail to grasp objects or use as a weapon. He can control other dinosaurs with his mind.

— POWER RATING —

Intelligence	●●●●●○○○
Strength	●●●●●●○○
Speed	●●●○○○○○
Durability	●●●●●○○○
Energy Projection	●●○○○○○○
Fighting Skill	●●●●○○○○

Reptiles on a Rampage

Stegron forced Dr. Curt Connors to restore dinosaurs to life using the remains found in a New York City museum. Dr. Connors then transformed into the Lizard and attacked Stegron, forcing Spider-Man to work overtime to contain the damage caused by the two reptilian combatants.

Plates on his back give Stegron additional protection.

His thick hide cannot be pierced by most weapons.

STILT-MAN

WEB FILE
The legs of Stilt-Man's armored, hydraulic suit can extend to hundreds of feet, and can also be used as battering rams. His suit enhances his strength, durability, and speed.

— POWER RATING —

Intelligence ●●●●●○○○○○
Strength ●●●●●○○○○○
Speed ●●●○○○○○○○
Durability ●●●●●○○○○○
Energy Projection ●●●○○○○○○○
Fighting Skill ●●●●○○○○○○

Stilt-Man Wilbur Day is famous for his unique armoured battlesuit. The suit's extendible legs allow Stilt-Man to reach the upper stories of the city's highest skyscrapers, but also leaves him vulnerable to tripping – a flaw frequently exploited by both Spider-Man and Daredevil.

The suit also contains an arsenal of weapons.

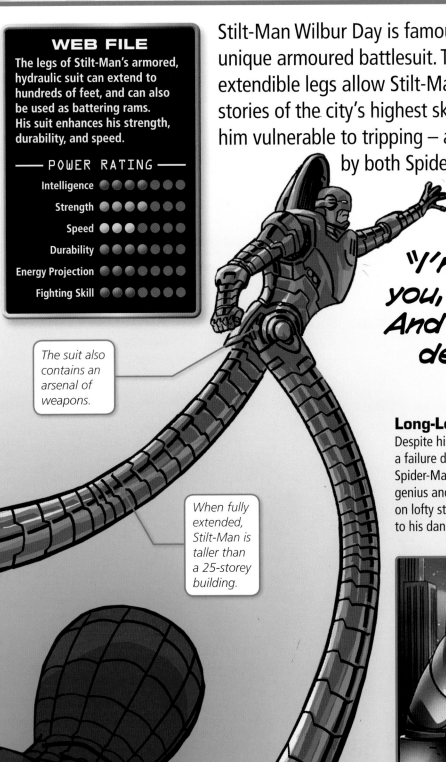

When fully extended, Stilt-Man is taller than a 25-storey building.

"I'm ready for you, Spider-Man! And this time I'm deadlier than ever!"

Long-Legged Loser
Despite his talents, Stilt-Man considers himself a failure due to his unremarkable criminal career. Spider-Man thinks Stilt-Man is an engineering genius and is wasting his potential by focusing on lofty stunts, but is always ready to put a stop to his dangerous rampages.

Stilt-Man's battlesuit provides enhanced strength and encases him in a bulletproof shell, though he is still vulnerable to getting knocked off balance.

STUNNER

Working for a company owned by Doctor Octopus, meek Angelina Brancale became a test controller for an experimental, hard light hologram. While her real body remained plugged into a machine, Angelina relished her new identity as the gorgeous, superpowerful Stunner and happily carried out Doc Ock's vendetta against Spider-Man.

In love with Doctor Octopus for giving her the life she dreamed of, Stunner lashed out at anyone who might hurt him – like Spider-Man!

Stunner can lift a car with ease.

New Confidence

Ignored owing to her plain looks, Angelina turned heads as the dazzling Stunner. Her aggressive flirting turned to violence whenever her advances were ignored. Spidey found her hard to defeat because she could vanish from the scene, back to her real body, in a flash.

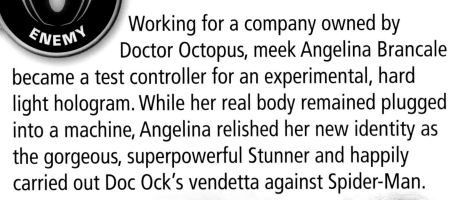

WEB FILE

Doctor Octopus's virtual reality (VR) technology gave Angelina beauty and power as Stunner, with superhuman strength, durability, agility, and senses.

— POWER RATING —

Intelligence ●●○○○○○○○
Strength ●●●●●○○○○○
Speed ●●○○○○○○○○
Durability ●●●●●●○○○○
Energy Projection ●○○○○○○○○○
Fighting Skill ●●●○○○○○○○

SUE RICHARDS

WEB FILE

As Invisible Woman of the Fantastic Four, Sue can make herself or other objects invisible and project invisible force fields that can also enable her to fly.

— POWER RATING —

Intelligence	●●●●●○○○○○
Strength	●●●○○○○○○○
Speed	●●●○○○○○○○
Durability	●●●●●○○○○○
Energy Projection	●●●●●●●○○○
Fighting Skill	●●●●○○○○○○

Sue Richards is the most powerful member of the Fantastic Four. The sister of Johnny Storm (the Human Torch), Sue married Reed Richards (Mister Fantastic). Sue welcomed Spider-Man into the Fantastic Four during its brief time as the Future Foundation.

The unstable molecules in Sue's costume allow it to change its appearance.

Sue can become completely invisible at will.

"You're entirely too clever, and adorable, to be fighting with us!"

Family Togetherness

The Invisible Woman is the person who unites the often-bickering members of the Fantastic Four. She is quick to accept others into the fold and has long viewed Spider-Man as a friend of the family. Sue recommended Spidey for her husband Reed Richards's Future Foundation, a think-tank seeking a better future for the world.

Sue is the most constant member in the Fantastic Four's changing lineup, giving her a depth of experience at dealing with trouble that no other member can match.

SWARM

Former Nazi scientist Fritz von Meyer came to a bad end when the killer bees he studied turned on him. Somehow his consciousness survived and he lived on as the swarm's guiding intelligence. Swarm views Spider-Man as a predator of insects, and so considers him his natural enemy.

Driven mad over the decades, Swarm hopes to reclaim his former glory with the insects he controls with his mind.

Hive of Evil

Resurrected during a science experiment at Empire State University, Swarm attacked the campus with his legions of killer bees. Peter Parker changed into his Spider-Man costume to battle the threat, only succeeding when he unleashed a chemical concoction that resembled insect repellent.

"On my command, slay the one called Spider-Man!"

When Swarm attacks, Spider-Man better stay on the move.

Swarm's true body is merely a skeleton.

WEB FILE

Swarm's body is made up of thousands of bees and, controlled by von Meyer's formidable intelligence, can take any shape. Swarm can control bees and other insects.

— POWER RATING —

Intelligence ●●●●●○○○
Strength ●○○○○○○○
Speed ●●●○○○○○
Durability ●●●●●○○○
Energy Projection ●●●○○○○○
Fighting Skill ●●●●○○○○

TARANTULA

Tarantula teamed with other villains to attack Spidey when he was powerless. Luckily, he got his powers back!

As the Tarantula, Anton Miguel Rodriguez worked as an assassin for the rulers of the tyrannical regime ruling his South American homeland of Delvadia. His cruel actions led to clashes with Spider-Man.

Spidey has to beware Tarantula's deadly touch.

WEB FILE

Tarantula's military training gave him fighting skills that were then enhanced by drugs. His boots were fitted with blades coated with a poison that could paralyze or kill.

— POWER RATING —

Intelligence ●●●●○○
Strength ●●●○○○
Speed ●●○○○○
Durability ●○○○○○
Energy Projection ○○○○○○
Fighting Skill ●●●●○○

Powering Up

Tarantula originally had no superpowered abilities, but he was injected with drugs that enhanced his strength and fighting skills. He used his new powers to track down and kill refugees from Delvadia in New York. Spider-Man stopped him.

Tarantula's retractable boot spikes are venomous.

TASKMASTER

Tony Masters – Taskmaster – has worked as a high-priced mercenary and physical trainer for heroes and villains alike. He'll take any job as long as he gets paid. Taskmaster is an expert with every type of weapon and has mastered all known fighting styles.

WEB FILE
Born with "photographic reflexes", Taskmaster can perform any combat move after seeing it once – even Spider-Man's acrobatics! He can mimic voices and use various weapons.

— POWER RATING —

Intelligence	●●●●●○○○○○
Strength	●●●○○○○○○○
Speed	●●○○○○○○○○
Durability	●●●○○○○○○○
Energy Projection	●○○○○○○○○○
Fighting Skill	●●●●●●●○○○

Taskmaster displays his expertise with all sorts of weapons.

"I'm a businessman. An educator."

Master of All Trades
Taskmaster is a familiar presence among both the Super Hero and Super Villain communities. Despite his super-powers Spider-Man can be beaten by Taskmaster in one-on-one combat, thanks to Taskmaster's encyclopedic knowledge of the fighting styles of everyone from Captain America to Boomerang.

Thanks to his ability to copy anyone's moves, Taskmaster is evenly matched against Captain America.

THING

WEB FILE

Cosmic radiation gave Ben a rocky hide and massive superhuman strength, stamina and durability. An exceptional pilot and trained astronaut, he also has great fighting skills.

— POWER RATING —

Intelligence ●●●●●●○○○○

Strength ●●●●●●●●●○

Speed ●●○○○○○○○○

Durability ●●●●●●●●○○

Energy Projection ●○○○○○○○○○

Fighting Skill ●●●●●●○○○○

Ben Grimm is the Thing, trapped in an unbreakable body of rock ever since the outer-space accident that created the Fantastic Four. The Thing has a big heart and acts as a "big brother" to less experienced heroes. He once teamed up with Spider-Man to stop an out-of-control Hulk.

Solid as a Rock

The Thing is a good-natured presence in the Super Hero community. For years he has run a friendly series of card games where Spider-Man and other heroes can let off steam, get advice from more experienced crime fighters, and share stories of their adventures.

"It's clobberin' time!"

Thing knows Spidey well and tolerates his wacky humour.

185

THOR

The God of Thunder and a founding member of the Avengers, Thor is an awe-inspiring figure who sets a heroic ideal for Spider-Man to live up to. Sent to Earth from Asgard by his father Odin, Thor became one of our world's most famous defenders despite the scheming interference of his arch-enemy Loki.

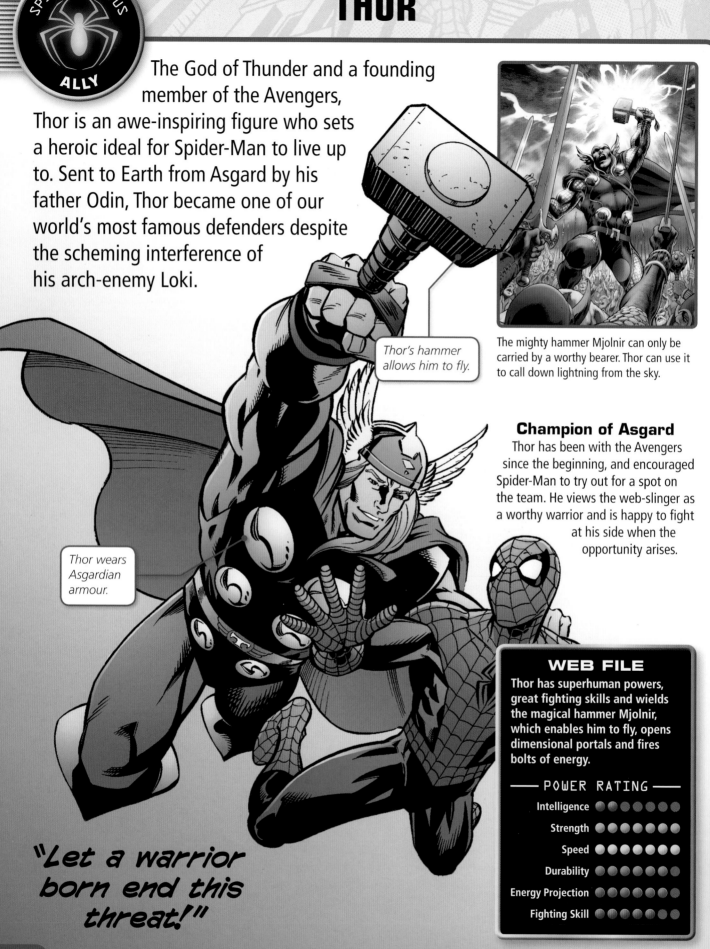

The mighty hammer Mjolnir can only be carried by a worthy bearer. Thor can use it to call down lightning from the sky.

Thor's hammer allows him to fly.

Thor wears Asgardian armour.

Champion of Asgard

Thor has been with the Avengers since the beginning, and encouraged Spider-Man to try out for a spot on the team. He views the web-slinger as a worthy warrior and is happy to fight at his side when the opportunity arises.

"Let a warrior born end this threat!"

WEB FILE

Thor has superhuman powers, great fighting skills and wields the magical hammer Mjolnir, which enables him to fly, opens dimensional portals and fires bolts of energy.

— POWER RATING —

Intelligence	●●●●●○○
Strength	●●●●●●●
Speed	●●●●●●○
Durability	●●●●●●●
Energy Projection	●●●●●○○
Fighting Skill	●●●●●○○

THOUSAND

Carl King enjoyed bullying Peter Parker in high school. Then he discovered the radioactive spider that had given Peter his amazing powers and ate it. Carl hoped to become just like Spider-Man, but instead transformed into a *swarm* of spiders! Thousand used his knowledge of Spider-Man's secret identity to target Peter's friends.

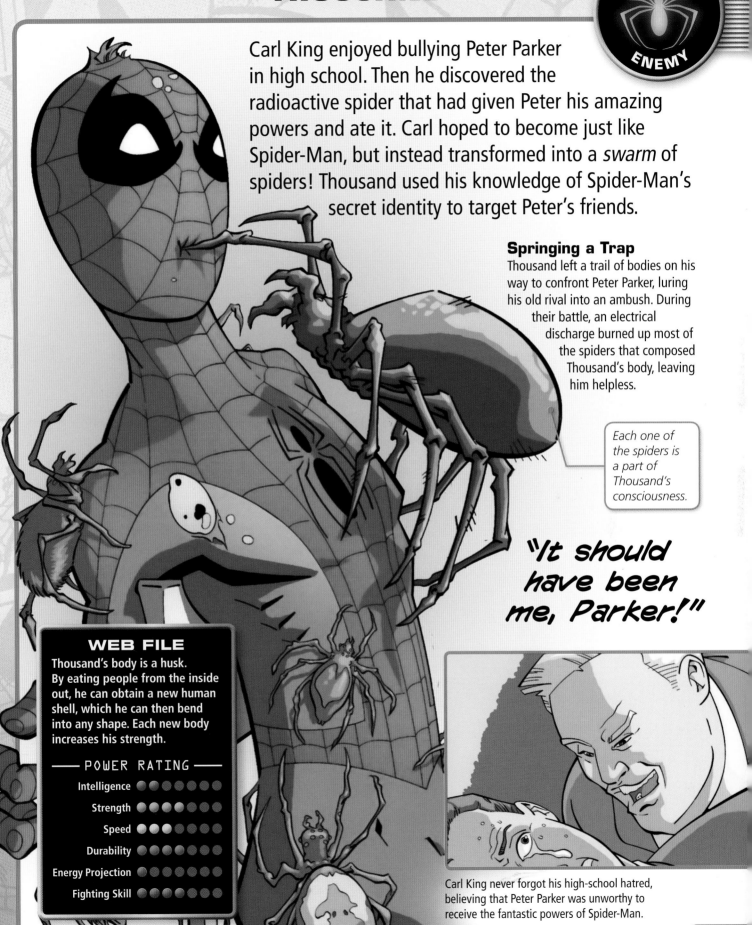

Springing a Trap
Thousand left a trail of bodies on his way to confront Peter Parker, luring his old rival into an ambush. During their battle, an electrical discharge burned up most of the spiders that composed Thousand's body, leaving him helpless.

Each one of the spiders is a part of Thousand's consciousness.

"It should have been me, Parker!"

WEB FILE
Thousand's body is a husk. By eating people from the inside out, he can obtain a new human shell, which he can then bend into any shape. Each new body increases his strength.

— POWER RATING —
Intelligence ●●●●●○○○○○
Strength ●●●●●●○○○○
Speed ●●●○○○○○○○
Durability ●●○○○○○○○○
Energy Projection ●○○○○○○○○○
Fighting Skill ●●●●○○○○○○

Carl King never forgot his high-school hatred, believing that Peter Parker was unworthy to receive the fantastic powers of Spider-Man.

The Tinkerer is highly sought after within the criminal underworld as a builder of gadgets, weapons, and vehicles. He encountered Spider-Man when creating high-tech gizmos to simulate an alien invasion. The Tinkerer has outfitted many of Spider-Man's foes, including the Beetle, Mysterio, Scorpion, and Trapster.

"My devices never fail!"

The Tinkerer's inventions are one-of-a-kind. Their effects are unpredictable, and so can be difficult for Spider-Man to combat.

Dangerous Everywhere
The Tinkerer has often landed behind bars, but that doesn't slow him down. Within the prison walls he is a king, offering his services to build devices for his fellow inmates and assist them in their escape attempts.

The Tinkerer sells his inventions to the highest bidder.

His body may be frail, but the Tinkerer's mind is as sharp as ever.

WEB FILE
Tinkerer is a scientific genius who specializes in making deadly, innovative weapons from ordinary machine parts.

— POWER RATING —
Intelligence	●●●●●●○
Strength	●●○○○○○
Speed	●●○○○○○
Durability	●●○○○○○
Energy Projection	●●●○○○○
Fighting Skill	●●●●○○○

SPIDEY STATUS
ENEMY

TOAD

WEB FILE

Toad can make superhuman leaps and is an extremely flexible, agile combatant. He can extend his tongue over 9 metres in length and use it as a whip in combat situations.

— POWER RATING —

Intelligence ● ● ● ● ○ ○ ○
Strength ● ● ● ● ○ ○ ○
Speed ● ● ● ○ ○ ○ ○
Durability ● ● ● ● ○ ○ ○
Energy Projection ● ○ ○ ○ ○ ○ ○
Fighting Skill ● ● ● ● ○ ○ ○

Orphan mutant Mortimer Toynbee developed the freakish ability to make tremendous leaps and lash out at foes with his elastic, prehensile tongue. As misfit loner Toad, he joined X-Men enemy Magneto's Brotherhood of Evil Mutants for a while. Spider-Man tried to boost Toad's self esteem to make him more likeable..

"I've never had a friend in my life."

A Jester's costume indicates toads sidekick status.

Toad's tongue can grasp objects, but this ability wasn't enough to win respect from heroes or villains.

Hoping for More

Toad formed a Super Hero team, the Misfits, with his fellow outcasts Frog-Man and Steel Spider. Unfortunately, the team didn't impress. Toad continued to look for new ways to apply himself, and eventually fell back in with his old comrades in the Brotherhood of Evil Mutants.

Toad's legs have incredible leaping power.

TOMBSTONE

A towering albino with a vicious streak and teeth filed into sharp points, Lonnie Lincoln carved out a fearsome reputation as mob hitman Tombstone. Robbie Robertson of *The Daily Bugle* had lived in fear of Lonnie since they were childhood friends, but his evidence finally saw that Tombstone was put behind bars for his crimes.

"My name is Tombstone. Just Tombstone. Am I clear?"

As a underworld enforcer in New York City, Tombstone hopes to finish Spider-Man once and for all.

Hands can crush a victim's skull.

Strength-enhanced muscles.

Vendetta

In retaliation for his prison sentence, Tombstone did everything he could to make Robbie's life a nightmare. Spider-Man helped his friend stay out of Tombstone's clutches, though the villain remained a constant threat among the city's criminal elite.

Quick reflexes from a lifetime of street fighting.

WEB FILE

Tombstone has superhuman strength and bulletproof skin thanks to a chemical concoction. He is an expert with guns and at hand-to-hand fighting.

— POWER RATING —

Intelligence	●●●●●○○
Strength	●●●●●●○
Speed	●●●○○○○
Durability	●●●○○○○
Energy Projection	●○○○○○○
Fighting Skill	●●●●●○○

TOXIN

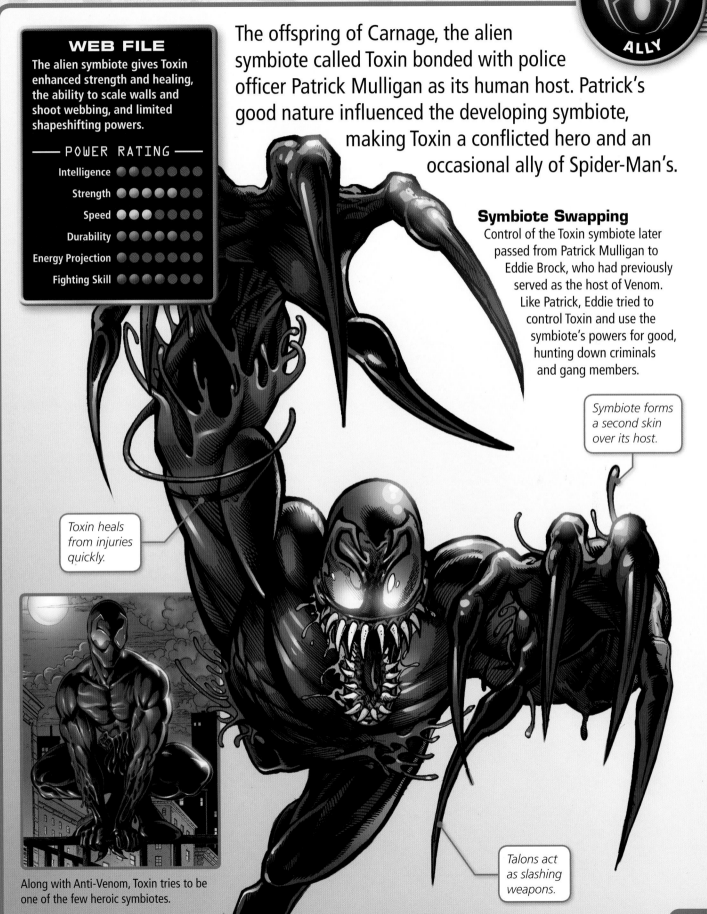

WEB FILE

The alien symbiote gives Toxin enhanced strength and healing, the ability to scale walls and shoot webbing, and limited shapeshifting powers.

— POWER RATING —

Intelligence ●●●●○○○○○○
Strength ●●●●●○○○○○
Speed ●●●○○○○○○○
Durability ●●●●●●○○○○
Energy Projection ●●●●○○○○○○
Fighting Skill ●●●●●○○○○○

The offspring of Carnage, the alien symbiote called Toxin bonded with police officer Patrick Mulligan as its human host. Patrick's good nature influenced the developing symbiote, making Toxin a conflicted hero and an occasional ally of Spider-Man's.

Symbiote Swapping

Control of the Toxin symbiote later passed from Patrick Mulligan to Eddie Brock, who had previously served as the host of Venom. Like Patrick, Eddie tried to control Toxin and use the symbiote's powers for good, hunting down criminals and gang members.

Symbiote forms a second skin over its host.

Toxin heals from injuries quickly.

Talons act as slashing weapons.

Along with Anti-Venom, Toxin tries to be one of the few heroic symbiotes.

TRACER

Tracer is a robotic lifeform that claims to be a "machine god", worshipped by other machines. Because machines have grown more sophisticated with each passing year, Tracer believes its power will grow and grow. Spider-Man defeated Tracer and its plans for world conquest, but it won't stay quiet forever.

Tracer's mind is connected to the world's computer systems. He gains additional knowledge instantly.

Deception

After Spider-Man foiled an attempt by Tracer to bomb New York City, Tracer tried to get revenge on Spidey by entering Avengers Tower and chatting with Peter's Aunt May. He claimed to be a member of the reserve Avengers, but when Aunt May grew suspicious, Tracer attacked! Spider-Man arrived just in time to stop him.

"The longer I operate, the stronger I become."

Bullets fired from Tracer's guns always find their target.

Armour protects Tracer's current body.

WEB FILE

Tracer can control machines and fire homing bullets that follow their targets. He has enhanced senses due to cyborg implants.

POWER RATING

Intelligence	●●●●●●●○
Strength	●●●●●○○○
Speed	●●○○○○○○
Durability	●●●●●○○○
Energy Projection	●●●●●○○○
Fighting Skill	●●●●●○○○

TRAPSTER

Scientist Peter Petruski, a specialist at inventing sticky substances, was formerly the third-rate crook Paste-Pot Pete. He underwent a Super Villain makeover to become Trapster. A frequent enemy of Spider-Man and the Human Torch, Trapster often works with other criminals as one of the Frightful Four.

If Spider-Man is hit by one of Trapster's blasts, he'll be glued in place.

Gift for Invention

Trapster is one of Spider-Man's most persistent foes. He has a lot in common with the web-slinger, being a chemical genius with a gift for building machines that spray adhesive fluids in the manner of Spider-Man's web-shooters.

Goggles protect eyes from adhesive fumes.

"Who traps the Trapster? No one!"

Pouch contains sticky grenades.

Glider provides a high vantage point.

WEB FILE

Trapster is a brilliant chemist whose glues and solvents allow him to walk up walls, immobilize enemies and fire sticky projectiles that explode on impact.

— POWER RATING —

Intelligence	●●●●●●
Strength	●●○○○○○
Speed	●●○○○○○
Durability	●●●○○○○
Energy Projection	●●●●○○○
Fighting Skill	●●●○○○○

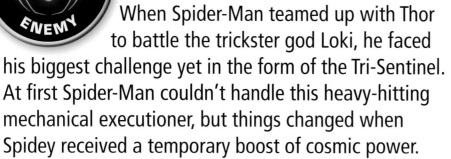

TRI-SENTINEL

When Spider-Man teamed up with Thor to battle the trickster god Loki, he faced his biggest challenge yet in the form of the Tri-Sentinel. At first Spider-Man couldn't handle this heavy-hitting mechanical executioner, but things changed when Spidey received a temporary boost of cosmic power.

Controlled by Loki, the Tri-Sentinel tried to destroy a nuclear power plant. Only Spider-Man stood in its way.

WEB FILE

Assembled from three mutant-hunting Sentinel robots, the Tri-Sentinel could topple buildings, fire energy beams, and automatically repair itself.

— POWER RATING —

Intelligence	●●●●●○○
Strength	●●●●●○○
Speed	●○○○○○○
Durability	●●●●●○○
Energy Projection	●●●●○○○
Fighting Skill	●●●○○○○

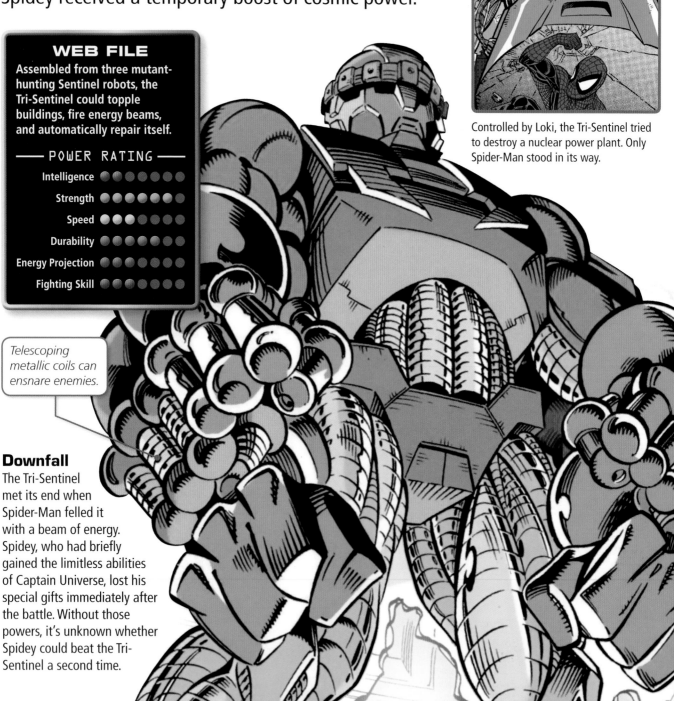

Telescoping metallic coils can ensnare enemies.

Downfall

The Tri-Sentinel met its end when Spider-Man felled it with a beam of energy. Spidey, who had briefly gained the limitless abilities of Captain Universe, lost his special gifts immediately after the battle. Without those powers, it's unknown whether Spidey could beat the Tri-Sentinel a second time.

UNCLE BEN PARKER

WEB FILE

Uncle Ben was a normal human being, but had had military training and was an above-average fighter for his age.

— POWER RATING —

Intelligence ●●●●●●●
Strength ●●●●●●●
Speed ●●●●●●●
Durability ●●●●●●●
Energy Projection ●●●●●●●
Fighting Skill ●●●●●●●

The Parkers never had much money, but Uncle Ben didn't let it show.

When Peter Parker's parents Richard and Mary died in a plane crash, Peter's Uncle Ben raised him as his own son. Ben and his wife May loved Peter and taught him the value of responsibility. Tragedy struck when, shortly after Peter gained his powers, he selfishly let a burglar go free – with terrible consequences for Ben.

Eternal Example

The burglar that Peter had ignored later killed Uncle Ben. Peter vowed that no one would ever suffer such a tragedy again, and committed himself to fighting injustice as Spider-Man! Uncle Ben has continued to serve as Peter's spiritual inspiration from beyond the grave.

"We'll bring him up like our own son."

The guilt he felt over his uncle's death led Peter to pursue a life of great responsibility.

VALERIA RICHARDS

The daughter of Reed and Sue Richards, Valeria Richards is a budding genius and one of Spider-Man's friends in the extended family that is the Fantastic Four. Doctor Doom assisted at Valeria's birth and secretly put a spell on her, which later allowed him to control her. Fortunately, Reed managed to break the spell.

WEB FILE

Valeria has a highly advanced intellect for her age and is considered a genius engineer and roboticist.

— POWER RATING —

Intelligence	●●●●●●●○○○
Strength	●●○○○○○○○○
Speed	●●○○○○○○○○
Durability	●●●○○○○○○○
Energy Projection	●●○○○○○○○○
Fighting Skill	●●●○○○○○○○

Unlimited Potential

Valeria is still developing her superpowers. Like her father, Reed Richards, she is showing early signs of genius-level intellect in a variety of fields. Peter Parker, who is a scientific genius himself, believes Valeria could be a scientist with Horizon Labs when she gets older.

The Thing has taught Valeria the basics of hand-to-hand combat.

"I knew those zombies weren't real, within 0.0000067 x 1058 margin of error!"

Despite growing up in the unusual environment that surrounds the Fantastic Four, Valeria is as down-to-earth and playful as a normal child her age.

VENOM

WEB FILE

The symbiote has enhanced strength and healing, as well as the ability to shoot webs and scale walls. Venom can control its composition for shapeshifting or camouflage purposes.

— POWER RATING —

Intelligence	●●●●●◦◦
Strength	●●●●●●◦
Speed	●●●◦◦◦◦
Durability	●●●●●◦◦
Energy Projection	●●●●◦◦◦
Fighting Skill	●●●●●◦◦

The alien symbiote known as Venom first entered Spider-Man's life as a black-and-white version of his costume. In time Spider-Man realized that his suit had a dark mind of its own! After Spider-Man rejected it, the suit bonded with disgraced reporter Eddie Brock to create Venom, an evil mirror of Spider-Man with shape-shifting abilities.

Host Hopping

The Venom symbiote has possessed other human hosts besides Eddie Brock. For a time it infected Mac Gargan, better known as the Scorpion. Most recently, Venom chose Peter Parker's friend Flash Thompson as its host. As Venom, Flash worked as an official agent of the U.S. military.

Shapeshifting lets Venom appear much larger than its human host.

Flash undertakes secret military missions wearing the Venom symbiote, but is only allowed to wear it for 48 hours at a time to prevent it from taking him over.

VERMIN

A mad scientist's experiment gave Edward Whelan fur, claws, and a heightened sense of smell. He became the rodent-faced villain Vermin, hiding in New York City's sewers and snatching victims for his dinner. Despite his crimes, Vermin desperately wishes to be cured of his rodent curse.

Vermin's claws and fangs harbour toxic bacteria.

When Vermin acts on animalistic instinct, he views all intruders as enemies and attacks without mercy.

Manipulated by Others

When Kraven the Hunter's daughter Ana lured Spider-Man into the sewer tunnels, Vermin tried to chase the intruders out of his territory. Though Vermin tries to keep a low profile, his ravenous hunger has caused him to prowl the city on the hunt for fresh meat.

Only a shred of humanity remains in Vermin.

WEB FILE

Vermin's powers are proportional to a man-sized rat. He can communicate with rats and summon them to do his will.

POWER RATING

Intelligence ●●●●●●●
Strength ●●●●●
Speed ●●●○
Durability ●●●
Energy Projection ●●
Fighting Skill ●●●

VINCENT GONZALES

Rookie N.Y.P.D. officer Vin Gonzales was Peter Parker's roommate and his rival for the affections of forensic detective Carlie Cooper. Acting on orders from high up in the department, Vin planted evidence to frame Spider-Man for murder.

Off-duty, Vin harboured resentment towards Spider-Man.

Justice Served

Vin eventually confessed to his role, and expressed regret over his part in the conspiracy. As a show of good faith he testified against his fellow plotters within the police force, receiving a reduced prison sentence in exchange for his cooperation.

WEB FILE

As a trained police officer, Vin Gonzales was in good physical shape with expertise in firearms and hand-to-hand combat.

— POWER RATING —

Intelligence	●●●○○○○
Strength	●●●○○○○
Speed	●●○○○○○
Durability	●●●○○○○
Energy Projection	●○○○○○○
Fighting Skill	●●●○○○○

After serving a reduced sentence, Vin hoped to rejoin the police force.

"Lying to a cop. I don't need that from my roommate."

As Peter Parker's roommate, Vin Gonzales quickly found his fate tied up with Spider-Man's. His involvement in a plan to take down the web-swinger backfired badly.

VULTURE

Wearing a flying harness he had invented, Adrian Toomes became the costumed criminal the Vulture. The Vulture was one of the first criminals Spider-man faced. He is old for a Super Villain, but his hatred of Spider-Man keeps him active. He is a frequent member of the Sinister Six villain team.

An electromagnetic harness allows the Vulture to fly.

The Vulture often enters a building by crashing through a window, using his wings to shield himself from flying glass.

"I've got to move fast, as only a vulture can!"

No Replacements Needed

Nothing bothers Adrian Toomes more than pretenders who try to claim the Vulture identity for themselves. Despite his advanced age, Toomes is still the best Vulture of them all, and he actively works to sabotage those who would take away his claim to fame.

Spider-Man is physically stronger, but can be outmanoeuvred by the Vulture.

WEB FILE

Adrian Toomes uses his electromagnetic harness to fly, and he can cut enemies with his sharp feathers. His harness also gives him enhanced strength.

— POWER RATING —

Intelligence	●●●●●○○
Strength	●●●●○○○
Speed	●●●○○○○
Durability	●●●○○○○
Energy Projection	●●○○○○○
Fighting Skill	●●●○○○○

WHIRLWIND

Born with super-speed, David Cannon put this power to use as the Human Top and later as the villain Whirlwind. A longtime foe of the Avengers, he is an occasional partner of Trapster, making him one of Spider-Man's many foes.

WEB FILE

When Whirlwind does one of his trademark spins, he can generate powerful gusts of wind or slash at his enemies with wrist-mounted blades.

— POWER RATING —

Intelligence
Strength
Speed
Durability
Energy Projection
Fighting Skill

Fresh Start

During a confrontation inside *The Daily Bugle* building, Spider-Man gave the former Human Top a new name, Whirlwind, while the two combatants traded insults. Whirlwind liked the name and fashioned a new identity.

Channeling the energy of a cyclone allows Whirlwind to fly.

When fighting Whirlwind, Spidey needs to watch for innocent bystanders who might be injured by flying debris.

"You haven't seen the last of me, hero!"

If he directs tornado-force winds at a target, Whirlwind can cause serious damage.

The leader of the notorious Dragon Lords gang in New York City's Chinatown district, White Dragon seeks alliances with powerful underworld figures like the Hood in order to keep his operations safe from Spider-Man.

WEB FILE

White Dragon can breathe fire or toxic gasses from his dragon's-head mask. He is a skilled hand-to-hand fighter who can slash enemies with his razor-sharp gloves.

── POWER RATING ──

Intelligence	●●●○○○○
Strength	●●○○○○○
Speed	○●○○○○○
Durability	●●○○○○○
Energy Projection	●●○○○○○
Fighting Skill	●●●○○○○

Pale-patterned costume conceals appearance.

Talons can pierce metal and slash enemies.

"Your period of grace is now over. The White Dragon is now forced to answer for you!"

As a surprise for attackers, the White Dragon's mask can release jets of flame or clouds of dangerous vapours.

Outmaneuvered in the Underworld

After Mister Negative made a move to control Chinatown, White Dragon tried to stop him. The fight didn't last long. The once-mighty White Dragon became a brainwashed pawn of Mister Negative, while Spider-Man tried to keep the gang war from spiraling out of control.

WHITE RABBIT

Lorina Dodson is completely mad, but she likes it that way! Obsessed with the book *Alice's Adventures in Wonderland*, she began her criminal career as the White Rabbit. Spider-Man knows that the White Rabbit is an unpredictable foe – her past antics have included riding a giant mechanical bunny.

The White Rabbit's crimes make sense in her head, but few others can predict what she'll do next.

Bunny ears are part of the gimmick.

Pocket watch can be swung as a weapon.

"Prepare to meet extinction at the hands of the White Rabbit gang!"

Expanding the Wonderland Gang

The White Rabbit is always looking for new recruits who fit her particular theme. During one crime spree she gave a new villain, the Walrus, a chance to impress her and join her gang. Their robberies came to an end when they ran into Spider-Man, Leap-Frog, and Leap-Frog's son Frog-Man.

WEB FILE

While lacking super powers, the White Rabbit is a creative inventor with talents in engineering, robotics, and explosives. Her weapons are often ridiculous, but no less deadly for that fact.

--- POWER RATING ---

Intelligence	●●●●●○○○○○
Strength	●●●○○○○○○○
Speed	●○○○○○○○○○
Durability	●●○○○○○○○○
Energy Projection	●○○○○○○○○○
Fighting Skill	●●●●○○○○○○

203

WILL O' THE WISP

Researching the outer limits of the electromagnetic spectrum, Jackson Arvad experienced a life-changing accident that loosened the natural bond between his body's molecules. As Will O' The Wisp, he attacked Spider-Man on the orders of evil mastermind Jonas Harrow.

WEB FILE

Jackson can control his body's composition, giving him the powers of flight, intangibility, and light projection.

— POWER RATING —

Intelligence	●●●●●○○○○○
Strength	●●●●○○○○○○
Speed	●●●○○○○○○○
Durability	●●●●●○○○○○
Energy Projection	●●●●○○○○○○
Fighting Skill	●●●○○○○○○○

Finding His Own Way

Jackson later rebelled against his boss, Jonas Harrow, and decided to go into business for himself. Silver Sable recognized the usefulness of Will O' The Wisp's unique combination of powers. She offered him a place on the team of reformed villains called the Outlaws, a position that saw him fight alongside Spider-Man.

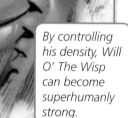

By controlling his density, Will O' The Wisp can become superhumanly strong.

"A million volts could pass through me and I wouldn't feel a thing!"

Will O' The Wisp can travel so quickly he appears as merely a streak of light, making it tough for Spidey to get a bead on him.

WOLVERINE

WEB FILE

Wolverine has a mutant healing factor and very sharp senses. His skeleton has been reinforced with unbreakable adamantium and he can extend razor-sharp claws from his fists.

—— POWER RATING ——

Intelligence	●●●●●○○○
Strength	●●●●●○○○
Speed	●●○○○○○○
Durability	●●●●○○○○
Energy Projection	●●●○○○○○
Fighting Skill	●●●●●●●○

James Howlett, Wolverine of the X-Men, is a friend that Spidey can count on. Born with a mutant healing factor, Wolverine received the upgrade of a metal skeleton with retractable claws through the top-secret Weapon X program. One of Spider-Man's New Avengers teammates, Wolverine is always the first into battle.

Experience Meets Enthusiasm
Wolverine's gruff personality might seem at odds with Spider-Man's easy-going attitude, but the two of them make a great team. During Spider-Man's time with the New Avengers, Wolverine became good friends with Aunt May and Mary Jane Watson.

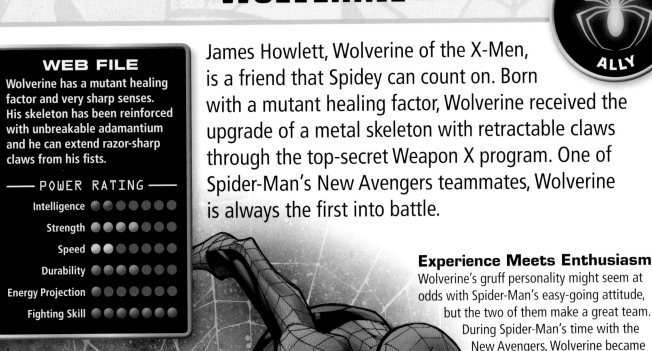

"I owe you some pain, bub!"

Enhanced senses make Wolverine a master tracker.

During their time as teammates, Spider-Man and Wolverine gained new appreciation for their different approaches to crime-fighting.

Thanks to a close encounter with Asgardian magic, four thugs gained the power to level anything in their path – and to make life miserable for heroes like Spider-Man!

Open for Business

The Wrecking Crew have tangled with both Spider-Man and Spider-Woman, but their greatest enemy is the Asgardian god of thunder, Thor. As their powers are magic-based, the Wrecking Crew's strength depends on the intensity of the mystical energies that flow to Earth from the realm of Asgard.

"We have more than enough power to steal big and live large!"

Forever a team, the members of the Wrecking Crew are always on the lookout for their next big heist.

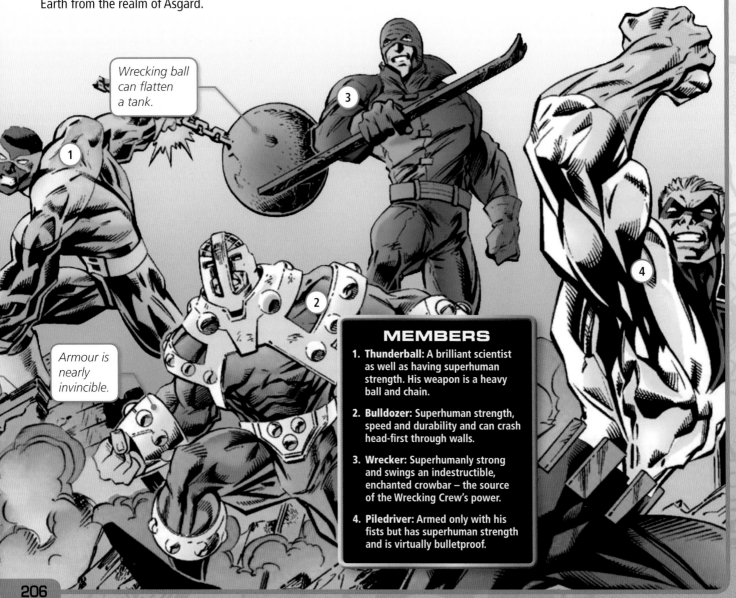

Wrecking ball can flatten a tank.

3

1

Armour is nearly invincible.

2

4

MEMBERS

1. **Thunderball:** A brilliant scientist as well as having superhuman strength. His weapon is a heavy ball and chain.

2. **Bulldozer:** Superhuman strength, speed and durability and can crash head-first through walls.

3. **Wrecker:** Superhumanly strong and swings an indestructible, enchanted crowbar – the source of the Wrecking Crew's power.

4. **Piledriver:** Armed only with his fists but has superhuman strength and is virtually bulletproof.

ZZZAX

Zzzax came into existence when the electricity released from a sabotaged power plant took on a mind of its own. The more power Zzzax drains, the stronger it gets. When Spider-Man's enemy Electro staged a prison break, he used Zzzax to help clear the way.

"Must have more!"

Zzzax feeds on energy and can release it in destructive waves across entire city blocks.

Force of Nature
Zzzax is capable of speech and possesses a limited form of intellect. During Spider-Man's first assignment with the New Avengers, he faced the threat of Zzzax during the mass breakout from the Raft, a maximum security penitentiary on an island in New York City.

Zzzax's primitive intellect means that it can't be reasoned with.

Incinerates its victims, and absorbs the electricity from their brains.

WEB FILE
Zzzax is a towering being of pure energy. The creature can fire incredible destructive blasts and is virtually impossible to attack.

— POWER RATING —
Intelligence	●●○○○○○
Strength	●●●●●○○
Speed	●●○○○○○
Durability	●●●●○○○
Energy Projection	●●●●●●○
Fighting Skill	●●●○○○○

Senior Editor Alastair Dougall
Editor David Fentiman
Editorial Coordinator Clare Millar
Project Art Editor Owen Bennett
Senior Designer Mark Penfound
Design XAB Design
Design Managers Guy Harvey, Victoria Short
Managing Editor Sadie Smith
Pre-Production Producer Kavita Varma
Producer Mary Slater
Creative Manager Sarah Harland
Publishing Manager Julie Ferris
Art Director Lisa Lanzarini
Publishing Director Simon Beecroft

This edition published in 2017
First published in Great Britain in 2014
by Dorling Kindersley Limited
80 Strand, London WC2R 0RL

A Penguin Random House company

002-193684-Oct/2017

A CIP catalogue record for this book is available from the British Library.

ISBN: 978-0-2413-3018-0

Printed and bound in China

marvel.com
© 2017 MARVEL

www.dk.com

A WORLD OF IDEAS:
SEE ALL THERE IS TO KNOW